A Handbook of Czechoslovak Genealogical Research

by

Daniel M. Schlyter

GENUN PUBLISHERS
789 South Buffalo Grove Road
Buffalo Grove, Illinois 60089

Grateful acknowledgement is made to the
Genealogical Library of the Church of
Jesus Christ of Latter-day Saints for
its cooperation and the use of various
materials.

Copyright © 1985 by Daniel M. Schlyter

First Printing, April 1985
Second Printing, March 1986
Third Printing, September 1987
All rights reserved.

International Standard Book Number: 0-912811-02-1.

Library of Congress Catalog Card Number: 85-70512.

Printed by Press America, Provo, Utah

TABLE OF CONTENTS

	Page No.
CHAPTER 1. BEGINNING YOUR RESEARCH	1
CHAPTER 2. HISTORY AND GEOGRAPHY	4
EARLY HISTORY	4
THE REFORMATION	7
COUNTER-REFORMATION	8
BIBLIOGRAPHY	10
CHAPTER 3. IMMIGRATION	11
BIBLIOGRAPHY	15
CHAPTER 4. DETERMINING THE PLACE OF ORIGIN	18
HOME SOURCES	18
LDS GENEALOGICAL INDEXES	22
A. International Genealogical Index	22
B. Family Group Records Archives	24
C. The Temple Records Index Bureau	24
VITAL RECORDS	24
A. Church	24
B. Civil	26
CEMETERY RECORDS	26
CENSUS RECORDS	26
NATURALIZATION	28
EUROPEAN PASSENGER LISTS	29
UNITED STATES PASSENGER LISTS	34
SOCIAL SECURITY RECORDS	35
LOCAL NEWSPAPERS AND PERIODICALS	36
STATE AND LOCAL HISTORIES	37
MILITARY RECORDS	38
WORLD WAR I DRAFT REGISTRATION RECORDS	38
OCCUPATIONAL AND FRATERNAL RECORDS	40
PASSPORT APPLICATIONS	42

CHAPTER 5.	LOCATING THE ANCESTRAL HOME	43
	GAZETTEERS	44
	A. *Administratives Gemeindelexikon der Čechoslovakischen Republic* [Administrative Gazetteer of the Czechoslovak Republic]........	44
	B. *Gemeindelexikon der in Reichsrate vertretenen Königreiche und länder* [Gazetteer of the Crownlands and Territories Represented in the Imperial Council]	47
	C. *Magyarország Helységnévtára* [Gazetteer of Hungary]	50
	D. *Názvy obcí na Slovensku za ostatných dvesto rokov* [Place Names in Slovakia During the Last 200 years]	52
	E. Other Gazetteers	54
	F. Duplicate Place Names	55
	MAPS	55
	THE DISTRICTS OF BOHEMIA, MORAVIA, AND SILESIA	61
CHAPTER 6.	GENEALOGICAL RESEARCH BY CORRESPONDENCE	65
CHAPTER 7.	SOURCES IN CZECHOSLOVAKIA	78
	VITAL RECORDS	78
	CENSUS RETURNS	84
	A. The 1828 Hungarian Census	85
	B. The 1848 Hungarian Census of Jews	85
	C. The 1857 Hungarian Census	87
	D. The 1869 Hungarian Census	87
	TAX LISTS	87
	LOCAL HISTORIES	88
	OTHER SOURCES	88

CHAPTER 8. LANGUAGES	90
CZECH AND SLOVAK LANGUAGES	91
A. Pronunciation	93
B. Grammar	94
Czech Word List	96
Slovak Word List	97
Months	98
Days of the Week	98
Numbers	98
Dates	100
GERMAN LANGUAGE	100
The German Alphabet	101
German Word List	102
Numbers	102
Months	103
LATIN LANGUAGE	103
Masculine and Feminine Names	103
Latin Word List	103
Numbers	104
HUNGARIAN LANGUAGE	105
Hungarian Word List	105
APPENDIX A. CZECHOSLOVAK GIVEN NAMES	106
APPENDIX B. PARISH INVENTORIES	115
APPENDIX C. MICROFILM NUMBERS FOR THE 1869 CENSUS OF ZEMPLÉN AND PART OF ESZTERGOM COUNTY	117

LIST OF ILLUSTRATIONS

		Page No.
1.	THE CREATION OF CZECHOSLOVAKIA	5
2.	AUSTRO-HUNGARY IN 1900	6
3.	THE SAME REGION AFTER WORLD WAR II	6
4.	DISTRIBUTION OF CZECHS IN THE UNITED STATES IN 1910	14
5.	EMIGRATION FROM HUNGARY	15
6.	DEATH NOTICE	19
7.	BIRTH AND CHRISTENING CERTIFICATE ISSUED 1935	20
8.	RESIDENCY CERTIFICATE	21
9.	INTERNATIONAL GENEALOGICAL INDEX (IGI)	23
10.	UNITED STATES CENSUS RECORDS - FORMAT FOR YEARS 1880, 1900, AND 1910	27
11.	HAMBURG PASSENGER LIST INDEX	32
12.	HAMBURG PASSENGER LIST	33
13.	WORLD WAR I DRAFT REGISTRATION CARD REQUEST	39*
14.	CERTIFICATE OF REGISTRATION FOR AN ALIEN ISSUED BY THE DEPARTMENT OF LABOR	41
15.	ADMINISTRATIVES GEMEINDELEXIKON - EXAMPLE OF AN ENTRY.	46
16.	ADMINISTRATIVES GEMEINDELEXIKON - POLITICAL DISTRICT	46
17A.	GEMEINDELEXIKON VON MÄHREN - LEFT-HAND PAGE	48
17B.	GEMEINDELEXIKON VON MÄHREN - RIGHT-HAND PAGE	49
18.	GEMEINDELEXIKON VON MÄHREN - POLITICAL DISTRICT	51
19.	MAP GRID OVERVIEW (1:75,000) - AUSTRO-HUNGARIAN EMPIRE	56

20.	ENLARGED SECTION OF MAP GRID OVERVIEW	57
21.	OLD HUNGARIAN COUNTIES (MEGYE) NOW IN CZECHOSLOVAKIA AND THE SOVIET UNION	59
22.	THE DISTRICTS OF BOHEMIA (ČECHY), MORAVIA (MORAVA), AND CZECH SILESIA (SLEZSKO),1918-1938	60
23.	APPLICATION FOR INDIVIDUAL BIRTH/MARRIAGE/DEATH CERTIFICATE	68*
24.	APPLICATION FOR GENEALOGICAL RESEARCH FROM CZECHO- SLOVAKIA IN THE FORM OF RUNNING ACCOUNT	69*
25.	INDIVIDUALLY ISSUED CERTIFICATES ON FORMS NOW IN USE IN CZECHOSLOVAKIA	74
26.	FIRST PAGE OF A NINE-PAGE ARCHIVAL REPORT	75
27.	A BIRTH AND MARRIAGE RECORD FROM AN ARCHIVAL REPORT ..	76
28.	A PARISH REGISTER IN CZECH, 1643 - CHRISTENING	80
29.	A PARISH REGISTER IN LATIN, 1678 - MARRIAGES	80
30.	AN EXAMPLE REFLECTING THE DIVERSITY OF LANGUAGES USED IN CZECHOSLOVAKIA	81
31.	A JEWISH BIRTH REGISTER IN GERMAN, 1869	82
32.	1848 HUNGARIAN CENSUS OF THE JEWS	86
33.	AN AUSTRIAN MILITARY RECORD	89
34.	ARCHIVAL DISTRICTS FOR WHICH INVENTORIES HAVE BEEN PUBLISHED	116
35.	1869 HUNGARIAN CENSUS	118

*These illustrations are unnumbered and untitled in the text so that the forms may be photocopied and used by the reader.

CHAPTER 1

BEGINNING YOUR RESEARCH

Perhaps the most important lesson to be learned about Czechoslovak genealogical research is that it can be done! Many Czechoslovak-Americans may think that it surely is impossible to search out their roots in socialist Czechoslovakia. You could reason that most records might have been destroyed during the course of wars and revolutions or that the socialist government certainly would not allow such research. Lay all these fears aside! Records in Czechoslovakia have been preserved. The government has created an excellent archival system and welcomes research. More importantly, these imagined problems pale in comparison to the real ones this book was written to help you solve.

Start your research by getting as much information as you can from older aunts, uncles, cousins, grandparents, or other relatives. Plan a personal visit, if possible. If this is not possible, interview them by telephone. A good time to call is on Saturday or Sunday when the rates are lowest. Information can be obtained by writing letters, but a lot of valuable data will be missed because many people won't spend the time to write out detailed information. Some family members enjoy reminiscing about their ancestors and will have a wealth of colorful stories about the family. Some of the information offered may be vague and unreliable, but even fanciful traditions often contain an element of truth. Frequently, you will obtain a valuable clue, such as a name or locality, that could not be found elsewhere or that might be located only after considerable time, effort, and expense.

Make your own search for family Bibles, old photographs, documents, or other materials that provide information about your family. After locating and evaluating these home and family sources, you will want to expand your research to include examination of other records such as birth certificates, death and marriage records, land records, and others. Before you can begin researching the European part of your heritage, you must determine exactly which ancestors came from Europe and specifically where they were born or resided.

The American part of your genealogy often presents more formidable obstacles than the European part, largely due to the fact that America was a frontier society. Little concern was given to the recording of births, deaths, or marriages in

America until the beginning of the twentieth century. Those of Czechoslovak ancestry are fortunate because, in most cases, their ancestors came to this country within the last hundred years. This means that most researchers are spared one of the more difficult genealogical undertakings, that of doing early American research.

A serious problem for some researchers is to determine the actual name of their immigrant ancestor. Some immigrants, in their eagerness to be assimilated into their newly-adopted American culture, traded their difficult foreign names for American names. This occurred often with given names and to a lesser extent with surnames. Given names usually were simply translated to their American counterparts: Jan to John, František to Frank, or Kateřina to Catherine. Because some given names have no English translation, they were frequently changed to almost any similar sounding American name. A notable example is Václav, a most troublesome name. A number of immigrants changed it to a German or Latin form such as Wenzel, Venceslas, or Wenceslaus; but the majority seem to have simply thrown the name overboard, taking names like William, Wesley, Wendel, or even James, according to the whim of the bearer. A list of given names with translations is found in Appendix A.

The Americanization of surnames was not infrequent, but was not so widespread as some may believe. Sometimes the name change was simply a translation: Jablečik became Appleton, Krejčí was translated to Taylor, or Procházka to Walker. In many cases the immigrant would chose an American name that sounded similar to his Slavic name: Kořista became Corrister, Maršálek became Marshall, Hudec became Hudson, Nozíř became Norris, and Šimaček became Smack. One Nebraska politician modified his Lapaček to LaPache. The name Vančura, with a simple lifting of the pen, became Van Cura. Who would think that this was a Czech name and not an established New York Dutch name, as American as Vanderbilt or Roosevelt? Of course, many did not want to change their names. Some simply spelled their surname as they had in the old country. But because many letters of the Czech alphabet are pronounced differently than in English, there was often a drastic difference in pronounciation of the name, particularly when the diacritic marks were omitted. Therefore, some immigrants who were sensitive about the pronunciation of their names changed the spelling so that Americans could pronounce their names correctly. Kokoška was changed to Kokoshka, Kučera to Kuchera or Kuczera, Chudec to Hudetz, or Jelinek to Yellineck.

By using research sources available in the United States, especially family records and traditions, you must determine the correct name of your immigrant ancestor in order to connect him with his ancestral lines in Europe. Many problems can be solved by familiarity with the Czech or Slovak language and the rules that govern the spelling of surnames (see Chapter 8: Languages).

The chapters in this book are designed to help you connect your American lineage to your Czechoslovak heritage. They include discussions of the languages with which you will be working as well as the resources that are available to help you locate your ancestral home.

Many of the sources discussed throughout this book are available at the Genealogical Library of the Church of Jesus Christ of Latter-day Saints (Mormon) in Salt Lake City, Utah. This library, often referred to in this book as the Genealogical Library, is open to the public without charge. Reference librarians are available at the library to guide library patrons. Books in the Genealogical Library collection do not circulate on interlibrary loan. Many, however, have been microfilmed. Microfilms in the Genealogical Library may be ordered and used at any of the many branch genealogical libraries. The services of these branch libraries are available to anyone for a nominal fee to cover the cost of ordering microfilm copies from the main library. Many of the sources mentioned in this book also have film file numbers listed. Use these numbers when ordering desired material at a branch library. Remember, branch librarians are all volunteers; while some are quite knowledgeable on genealogical procedures, others are less experienced. It should not be expected that a librarian in a small branch library would be skilled in Czechoslovak research.

A list of branch libraries in your area may be ordered by writing to:

>Correspondence Section
>Genealogical Library
>35 North West Temple Street
>Salt Lake City, Utah 84150

The collection of the Genealogical Library includes genealogical reference material, vital records, and other primary source material from many parts of the world, especially from North and South America and Europe. For Czechoslovakia, the library has an excellent collection of gazetteers and other reference materials on microfilm, but no vital records or other primary sources have been microfilmed in the country. Negotiations are in progress for permission to microfilm genealogical source material in Czechoslovakia but, as yet, without success. It is interesting to note, however, that negotiations have been successful for microfilming records in neighboring Poland and Hungary. You may check with the library every year or so to determine whether Czechoslovak records have been obtained.

CHAPTER 2

HISTORY AND GEOGRAPHY

Czechoslovakia did not exist as a country until 1918 when it was created from parts of Austria and Hungary. The new Czechoslovak Republic consisted of the following three regions (see maps on pages 5 and 6):

1. The Czech lands, including the Czech-speaking Austrian provinces of Bohemia, Moravia, and Silesia, as well as a small section of Prussian Silesia.

2. The northern area of old Hungary, called Slovakia, inhabited by Slovak-speaking people. It is the combination of Czech and Slovak that yields the modern name, Czechoslovakia.

3. The northeastern section of old Hungary inhabited by people who speak Rusin, a Ukrainian dialect. This area, named Sub-Carpathian Russia or Ruthenia, was ceded to the Soviet Union after World War II.

EARLY HISTORY

The earliest recorded inhabitants of the area known today as Czechoslovakia were Celtic tribes, one of which was referred to by Roman historians as the Boii. The modern name for the province of Bohemia is derived from the name of this tribe, although the term is not used by the Czechs themselves. In the first and second centuries A.D., Slavic tribes moved westward into Poland; and, in the fifth century, Slavs first settled in the area south of the Carpathian mountain range. The legendary chieftain, Čech, led his tribe to the valley of the Vltava River. His name eventually was bestowed upon the land of Bohemia, which is called Čechy in the Czech language. Before the spelling reforms of the seventeenth century, this word was spelled Czechy, which accounts for the difficult English spelling of Czechoslovakia.

Many of the Slavic tribes of central Europe were united early in the seventh century under one leader, Samo, whose state seems to have been centered in Moravia. With the death of Samo in 658 or 659, his empire, the first distinctly Slavic state, disintegrated. In the ninth century, another powerful ruler, Mojmír I, succeeded in uniting several Slavic tribes. His

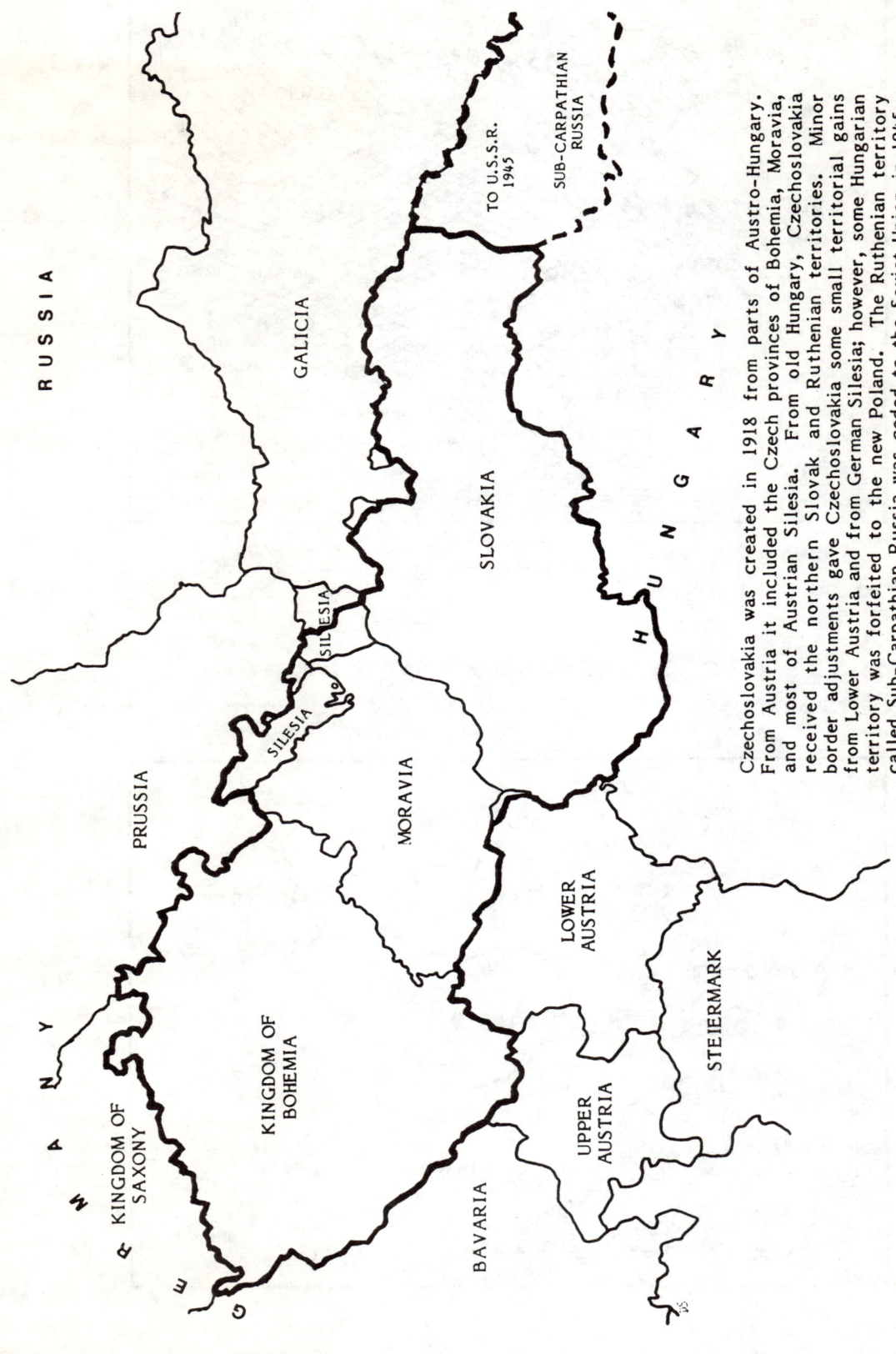

NO. 1. THE CREATION OF CZECHOSLOVAKIA.

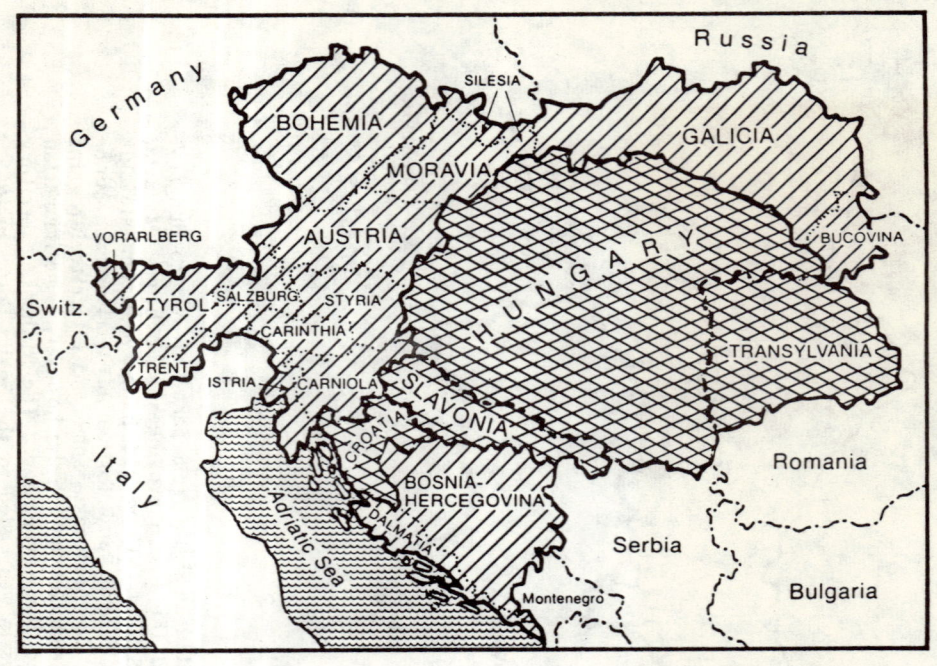

NO. 2. AUSTRO-HUNGARY IN 1900.

NO. 3. THE SAME REGION AFTER WORLD WAR II.

domains became known as the Great Moravian Empire and included not only Moravia but, ultimately, most of Slovakia and Austria, all of Bohemia, and Lusatia (a Slavic area of Saxony consisting of what is now the southeastern portion of East Germany and part of Poland).

The first-known Christian church among the western Slavs was established in the city of Nitra, Slovakia, in 833 or 835. Mojmir I had accepted Christianity from the German Bishop of Passau. Prince Rostislav, his successor as ruler of Great Moravia, fearing political domination by the German Holy Roman Empire and the Roman church, turned to the Eastern Orthodox religion and requested that the Byzantine Emperor send Christian missionaries. The prince was converted to Christianity by the Slav missionaries Cyril and Methodius in 863. Bořivoj, of the emerging Bohemian domain, was converted to Christianity by Methodius in 880. However, in 895 the Moravian princes promised their allegiance to the Holy Roman Empire in an effort to prevent invasion by the Magyars (Hungarians). The Byzantine church, with its Slovanic rite, was expelled and replaced by the Roman church and the Latin rite. Despite this alliance, the eastern area of Great Moravia, inhabited by the Slovaks, fell to the Hungarians in 896 and remained under their domination until 1918. This 1,000 years of Hungarian rule hindered the development of the Slovaks while their Czech brothers progressed unfettered, having the advantage of independence until 1620.

The great Moravian Empire was supplanted in the tenth century by the Duchy of Bohemia, which united the peoples of the Czech lands--Bohemia, Moravia, and Silesia. Bohemia fell within the framework of the Holy Roman Empire and was raised to the rank of kingdom in 1085. Under the Přemyslide dynasty, during the twelfth century, the prestige of the kingdom increased; and the king of Bohemia was installed as one of the electors of the emperor. This meant that the king of Bohemia himself could be elected emperor.

The male line of the Czech Přemyslide ruling house died out in 1306 and was replaced by the Luxemburg family. King John, son of the emperor, married the sister of the last Přemyslide king and claimed the Bohemian throne. His son, Charles I, took the throne in 1346. King Charles I of Bohemia later became Charles IV, Emperor of the Holy Roman Empire. His reign was a golden age for Bohemia. In 1348 he founded a university in Prague and, during his reign as emperor, Prague became the chief city of the empire--a city of splendor, culture, and learning.

THE REFORMATION

During the fifteenth century, followers of the religious reformer and martyr, Jan Hus, waged a war of defense against the crusading Catholic armies. The Hussite armies, which were led by Jan Žižka, won a series of brilliant victories against Catholic armies; and in 1436, at the Council of Basel, the Catholic church recognized followers of Hus as "true Christians and genuine sons of the church." The Hussites also were called "Utaquists," from the Latin phrase meaning "each of two," because they believed in partaking of both bread and wine in the communion. They never fully broke with the Roman church. Hussite priests, although allowed to marry, were consecrated by bishops of the Roman Catholic church. However, as a result of the Hussite movement, the Unity of Brethren [Jednota bratrská] group evolved. In the sixteenth century this group broke all ties with the Roman and Hussite churches and set up its own church and priesthood, thereby becoming the Protestant church of Bohemia. The movement was such a powerful force throughout the country that by the early 1600s the Czech lands had become a stronghold of Protestantism. The Hussite faith and the Brethren did not gain many followers among the Slovaks, but other forms of Protestantism did find many adherents in the northern Slovak counties of Hungary. The Germans and Slovaks who left the Catholic church usually became Lutherans, whereas Hungarians of similar persuasion usually became Calvinists, joining the Reformed church.

Jan Žižka

After the Hussite wars, the crown of Bohemia passed to a Czech, Jiří of Poděbrady, and from him to the Polish Jagellon dynasty, where it remained until 1526. Upon the death of the last Jagellon king, Ferdinand I of Habsburg was elected to the Bohemian throne. He was already ruler of Austria and was elected king of Hungary shortly after receiving the Bohemian crown, thereby bringing both the Czechs and Slovaks under the Habsburg rule.

COUNTER-REFORMATION

Much to the displeasure of its new Austrian Habsburg rulers who were devout Catholics, the Czech lands had become firmly entrenched as a Protestant nation. The struggle between Catholicism and Protestantism in Europe was the cause of the Thirty Years War (1618-1648) which erupted in Prague when Catholic officials of the king were bodily thrown out of a window by a Protestant delegation. In 1620 the Germanic Catholic armies of the Habsburg emperor defeated the Czechs at the Battle of White Mountain, just outside Prague. With this Austrian victory began an era of Germanization and harsh efforts to re-Catholicize the wayward Czech population. Conditions in the Czech lands were deplorable after the Battle of White Mountain. The total population was reduced by half; some were killed in the war and many went into exile. One third of the farmland was left untilled. New Catholic nobility of foreign origin, in cooperation with Austrian Catholic authorities repressed, everything Protestant and Czech. Beginning with the year 1624, the Catholic church became the only recognized church. Protestant clergy were expelled from the country, new Catholic clergy were brought in, and the Unity of the Brethren church was severely persecuted. Many of the Brethren either emigrated to Poland, Hungary, Holland, or Germany (from which some eventually emigrated to America) or converted to Catholicism. In time, however, the right to emigrate became a prerogative only of the nobility and inhabitants of royal cities. The common people were simply forced to convert to Catholicism. In many cases the conversion was only a pretense and, in spite of persecution, much of the nation remained faithful to the Protestant teachings. But within several generations, the fierce efforts of the Counter-Reformation produced an almost entirely Roman Catholic population.

Under the Habsburg rule, German became the official language of the land, and Czech was relegated to a peasant tongue that commanded little respect. At one point, it almost was threatened with extinction. All important government offices were transferred to Vienna. Bohemia, Moravia, and Silesia became mere provinces of Austria which, together with Hungary, constituted the Austro-Hungarian Empire.

Emigrants from the area now called Czechoslovakia traveled on Austrian passports and were counted as Austrians or Hungarians. Thus, the U.S. census and passenger lists usually record Czechs and Slovaks with the more general country of origin.

Germans had begun settling in the Czech lands soon after German Christianity was accepted, but it was the Přemyslide kings and their German princesses who brought large numbers of German craftsmen and colonists into the kingdom. Germans also settled in Slovakia, but the influx was greatest in the Czech lands where German communities predominated in the Sudeten border area and southern Moravia. The German population maintained its German language and culture and, in general, lived peaceably alongside its Slavic neighbors.

During the 1800s, the Czechs and Slovaks experienced a cultural and nationalistic awakening. Czech and Slovak languages were restored to a position of respect, developing into languages of literature and culture. With the defeat of Austria in World War I, these strong national feelings were acted upon. In 1918 the Czechs, Slovaks, and Ruthenians joined to create a new nation, the Czechoslovak Republic. This nation, a model of European democracy, remained a land of freedom throughout the troubled 1930s when the neighboring countries developed totalitarian dictatorships. Sadly, the democracy did not last.

In 1938 Hitler's German armies occupied the Czech lands under the pretense of unifying the German population living in the border areas of Bohemia with their fellow Germans in the Nazi Reich. Slovakia was set up as an independent state under the "protection" of Germany. In 1945 Slovakia and the Czech lands were "liberated" by the Soviet armies; and, as agreed upon by the Allied powers, Soviet "advisors" were allowed to remain in Czechoslovakia after the war. In 1948 the Communist Party of Czechoslovakia took control of the Czechoslovak government.

BIBLIOGRAPHY

Kaminsky, Howard. <u>A History of the Hussite Revolution</u>. Berkeley: University of California Press, 1967.

Oddo, Gilbert L. <u>Slovakia and Its People</u>. New York: Robert Speller and Sons, 1960.

Seton-Watson, Robert W. <u>A History of the Czechs and Slovaks</u>. London, 1943. Rpt. Hamden, Connecticut: Archon Books, 1965.

Thomson, S. Harrison. <u>Czechoslovakia in European History</u>. Revised ed. Hamden, Connecticut: Archon Books, 1965.

Wiskemann, Elizabeth. <u>Czechs and Germans, A Study of the Struggle in the Historic Provinces of Bohemia and Moravia</u>. 2nd ed. New York: St. Martin's Press, 1967.

Bride and bridesmaid in Moravian costume.

The Black Tower of the Prague Castle.

CHAPTER 3

IMMIGRATION

The first Czech immigrants to America came with the Dutch. The first known was Augustin Herrman who in 1633 arrived in New Amsterdam (later New York) with the Dutch East India Company. He was a man of good education, a surveyor by profession. In 1660 he left New York for Maryland where Lord Baltimore granted him 2,000 acres of land in recognition of his preparation of a map of "Virginia and Maryland as It Is Planted and Inhabited This Present Year 1670 Surveyed and Exactly Drawn by the Only Labour and Endeavour of Augustin Herrman, Bohemiensis." He called the estate "New Bohemia." Whether he planned to start a colony of his fellow countrymen is not known. There is no record of his having attracted other Bohemians to his "New Bohemia."

Augustin Herrman
The first known Czech immigrant in America.

Several other Bohemians are noted among the citizens of New Amsterdam, including Frederick Philipse, Adam Unbelka, and John Kostlo. There was also a Moravian named Jeurien (possibly Jiří) Fradell.

In the sixteenth century, Holland was a haven for religious dissidents and free-thinkers. This is why English Puritans spent many years in Holland before settling in America. Many members of the Unity of the Brethren faith fled a harsh, methodic persecution in the Czech lands and settled in Saxony, Poland, Holland, and anywhere else they were tolerated. It seems that a number of Czechs came to the Americas with the Dutch. That a trickle of Bohemians came is evident by the Czech surnames throughout the early colonies. These include such names as Barta, Duch, Donak, Doza, Marshelek, Hallek, Lumtra, and Standla. William Paca of Maryland, who was one of the signers of the Declaration of Independence, was of Czech extraction.

A small body of Moravian Brethren from Saxony landed in Georgia in 1736. Charles Wesley, who was the brother of John Wesley, the father of Methodism, attended the dedication of their church there. In 1740 they moved to Philadelphia and by 1741 they were settled in Bethlehem in Lehigh Valley, Pennsylvania. These Brethren were already quite Germanized, having lived in Saxony for a generation or more, and their Slavic impact on America was negligible.

Emigration from Austro-Hungary was essentially only a trickle until the 1840s. Until this time there was no economic stimulus for emigration. Also, permission to emigrate was almost impossible to obtain.

Early in the nineteenth century, Europe began to industrialize. The movement started in western Europe, but was slow to reach the eastern empire. Industrialization began in parts of Bohemia and Moravia with linen weaving and glassmaking. In Silesia, iron making and coal mining became important industries. People moved to the cities whenever possible, deserting the rural countryside for a better life.

The Industrial Revolution also brought capitalistic competition to the emerging industries of Slavic Austro-Hungary. British textiles and Swedish steel gave stiff competition. Cheap Polish wheat and a loss of market for flax hurt the farmers. The mid 1900s found many people increasingly eager to find work and success in America. The stifling political climate and dominance of the Catholic church in Austria prompted many to leave the Czech lands for religious and political reasons.

Emigration from Austro-Hungary was not a simple matter. First, the emigrant had to show that he was of good character and debt free. There were fees to pay, affidavits to obtain, and lots of paperwork. Not all emigrants were patient enough to wait for legal permission to leave, but leaving illegally was extremely difficult. The earliest large-scale emigration was of Bohemians and Moravians. These early emigrants went to Texas, Missouri, Illinois, and Wisconsin.

A few Czechs were in Texas as early as the 1820s, but settlement there began in earnest two decades later. In 1848 a Protestant pastor named Bergman, of Západov, Moravia, settled in Cat Spring, Texas, near Austin. He wrote letters with glowing reports of America to parishioners back home. These letters influenced a group of Moravian Brethren to go to Texas instead of southern Hungary which they had been considering. Another Moravian, Pastor Josef Zvolánek from Vsetín, also settled in Texas, encouraging other Moravian Protestants to follow. The influence of these early Texas immigrants made it a favored destination for later Moravian Protestants so that most Texans of Czech stock can trace their ancestry back to Moravia.

St. Louis, Missouri, for a time was a very important settling place for Czechs in America. It was an important river port, and early immigrants who stopped there encouraged others to follow. In 1854 St. Louis was the site of the first Czech church in America, the Church of St. John Nepomuk, and the second Czech-language newspaper. After 1853 St. Louis began to lose its preeminence as a Czech settlement as a result of the railroad reaching Chicago. Chicago at that time had only a small Czech community, but the convenience of rail travel and the encouragement from early settlers soon brought many more. The Czechs built St. Vaclav's church there in 1864. The railroad also contributed to the growth of the Czech community in Cleveland.

Czechs settled extensively in Wisconsin; Wisconsin encouraged the settlement of immigrants. Bohemians, as well as Poles, Germans, and Scandinavians, were eagerly solicited as settlers. Czechs began farming in Caledonia, on Lake Michigan near Racine, in 1844. Soon Czech settlers were found in Milwaukee, Kewaunee, Oconto, and Manitowoc counties. The first Czech-language newspaper in America, <u>Slovan Amerikánský</u>, was printed in 1860 in Racine, Wisconsin. In 1890 three-sevenths of Kewaunee county was of Bohemian extraction.

By the late 1800s, Iowa, Minnesota, Nebraska, Kansas, Oklahoma, New York, and the Dakotas had notable Czech communities. In 1900 Bohemians constituted 9% of all foreign-born inhabitants in Nebraska, 9% in New York, and 7% in Oklahoma. Many of the later immigrants became city dwellers. In 1880 the fifty largest cities of the United States held under 40% of the Bohemians in this country. By 1900 this figure had grown to 50%. This was caused by growing Czech colonies in Chicago (with over 25,000), Cleveland (7,000), New York City, and Baltimore. Extensive settlements also developed in St. Louis and Omaha.

Slovaks are not as easily accounted for. Early statistics lumped them together with Hungarians. They represented probably less than one-third of the Hungarian count. Slovak immigration

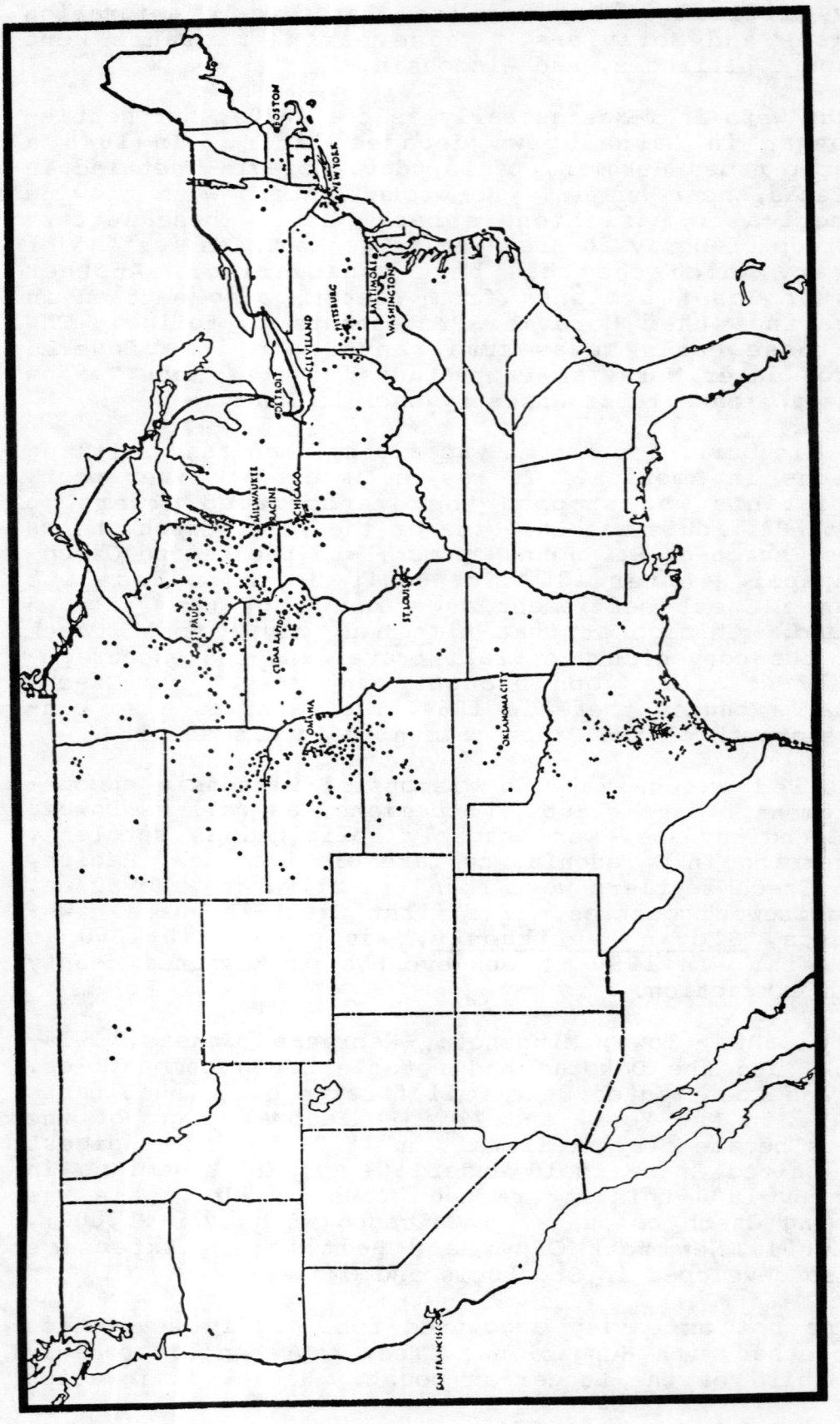

Each mark represents a settlement of more than 100 people of Czech birth or descent. [Source: Thomas Čapek, Čechs (Bohemians) in America (Boston: Houghton Mifflin Company, 1920).]

NO. 4. DISTRIBUTION OF CZECHS IN THE UNITED STATES, 1910.

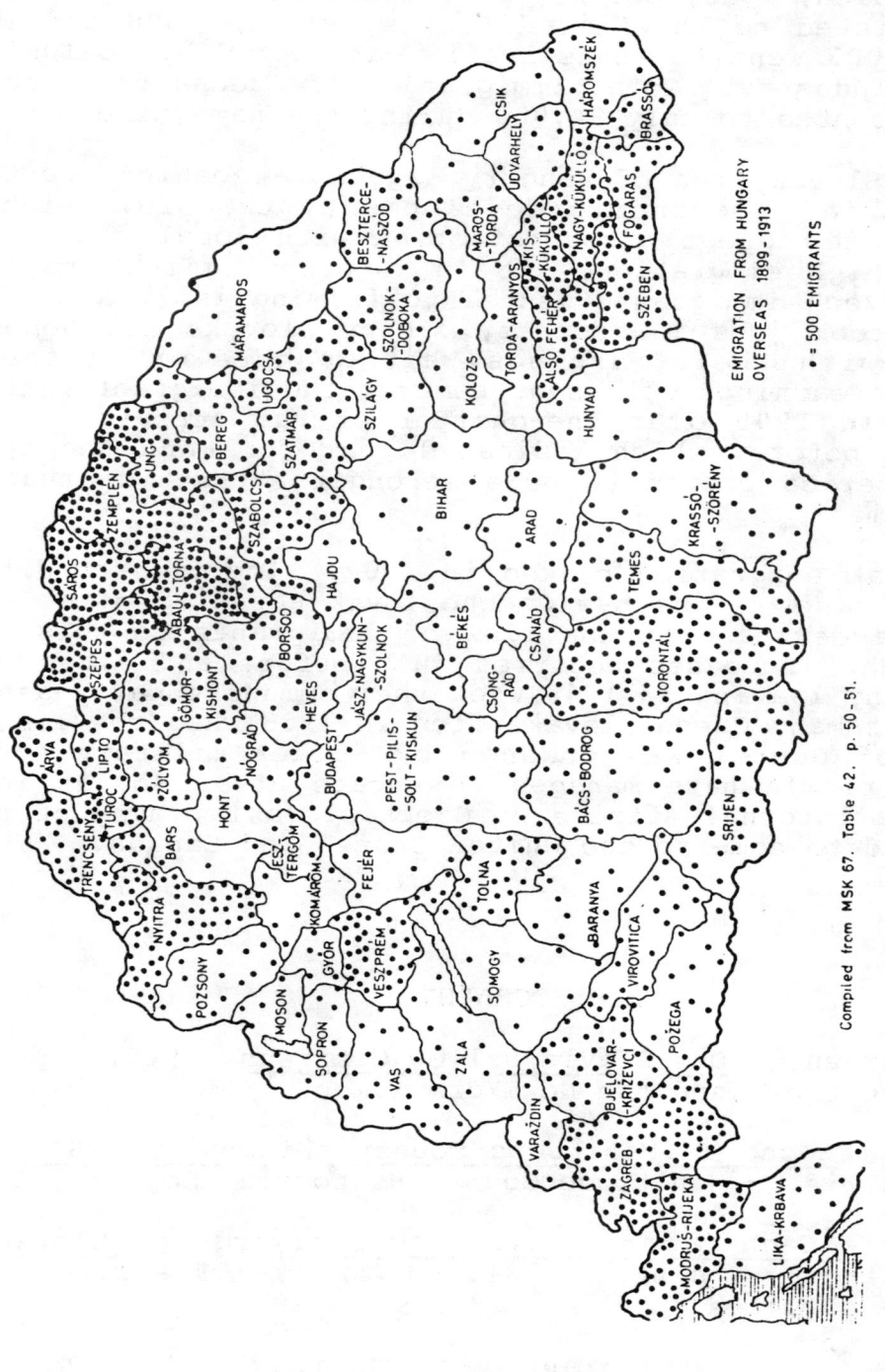

Note the comparatively high emigration from the northern counties of Hungary. These later constituted Slovakia and Sub-Carpathian Russia.

NO. 5. EMIGRATION FROM HUNGARY.

[Source: Julianna Puskás, *From Hungary to the United States (1880-1914)* (Budapest: Akadémiai Kaidó, 1982).]

to the United States at first lagged behind that of Czechs from Bohemia and Moravia but began rapidly increasing at the end of the nineteenth century, far surpassing Czech immigration by the turn of the century. Data from Annual Reports of Commissioner of Immigration (Balch, 1910, pp. 256-257) indicate that over 322,000 Slovaks immigrated to the United States between 1898 and 1908. Of these, 169,000 went to Pennsylvania, attracted by coal mining and the steel industry. Total immigration of Czechs from Bohemia and Moravia amounted to only 84,000 during the same time period.

Since the Slovak area of Hungary lagged far behind the Czech lands of Austria in economic development, the Slovak inhabitants experienced great dissatisfaction with local conditions, resulting in high emigration. It is interesting to note that, whereas many Czech immigrants went into farming in this country, most Slovaks took jobs in industry. Many Slovaks had hopes of buying farms with their earnings, either here or in the old country. Often earnings were sent home or the immigrant returned to Hungary. In 1905 over one-quarter of the arriving Slovaks had been here before, which indicated that for many the opportunities in America proved to be a stronger attraction than the longing for home.

Czechoslovak emigration peaked in 1907. Improved conditions in Europe and also in the new Czechoslovak Republic after World War I led to a decrease in the flow of immigrants to this country. Subsequent increases occurred just before and after World War II with many leaving in 1948 when the Communist party assumed power. A great many Czechoslovaks fled in 1968 when the liberalized regime of Dubček was crushed by Soviet military action. Only a tiny trickle have managed to escape after Soviet interference in the internal affairs of Czechoslovakia; many of these emigrants opted to come to the United States and Canada.

BIBLIOGRAPHY

Balch, Emily Greene. Our Slavic Fellow Citizens, 1910. Rpt. New York: Arno Press and the New York Times, 1969.

Benes, Frank. Czechs in Manitowoc County, Wisconsin, 1847-1932. Manitowoc, Wis.: Manitowoc County Historical Society, 1979.

Capek, Thomas. Čech Communities in America and The Slovaks in America, in one volume, 1921. Rpt. San Francisco: R&E Research Associates, 1969.

_____. The Čechs (Bohemians) in America, 1920. Rpt. New York: Arno Press and the New York Times, 1969.

Gellner, John and Smerik, John. The Czechs and Slovaks in Canada. Toronto: University of Toronto Press, 1968.

Hudson, Estelle. *Czech Pioneers in Southwest*. Dallas: Southwest Press, 1935.

Laska, Vera, ed. *The Czechs in America 1633-1977, A Chronology and Fact Book*. Ethnic Chronology Series #28. Dobbs Ferry, New York: Oceana Publications, 1978.

Rosicky, Rose, comp. *History of Czechs in Nebraska*. Omaha, 1929. Rpt. Evansville, Ind.: Unigraphic, 1977.

Roucek, Josef. *Czechs and Slovaks in America*. Cultural Mosaic Series. Lerner Publications, 1967.

Use the catalog of the Genealogical Library and other libraries to find other local histories. Also see:

Jerabek, Esther. *Czechs and Slovaks in North America: A Bibliography*. New York: Czechoslovak Society of Arts and Sciences in America, Inc., 1976.

Bohemian national costumes.

CHAPTER 4

DETERMINING THE PLACE OF ORIGIN

Once you have traced your family back to your immigrant ancestor, you will face what may be one of the most difficult problems of your research--determining exactly where the ancestor was from. Czechoslovakia has no central index of its genealogical records. Records of births and marriages in the Austro-Hungarian Empire were kept locally. In order to locate parish, civil, or other records needed for genealogical research, it is necessary to determine the specific place from which your ancestors originated. It can be a difficult task to find the place of origin for those who reached American soil in the first decades of the 1800s or earlier. The scanty records of that era seldom list a birthplace or former residence. Americans of Czechoslovak ancestry are fortunate, however, since most Czech and Slovak immigration occurred in the latter part of the nineteenth century and early twentieth century when record keeping was much improved over earlier times. Emigration, immigration, naturalization, census, and other records have been kept which can provide needed information. Other less obvious sources are available as well. This chapter discusses many different sources that may provide a birthplace* for your ancestor.

HOME SOURCES

One of the greatest sources of genealogical information about your ancestors is your own home and family. As discussed in Chapter 1, you should interview your relatives carefully, especially the older ones. Often the family will know of or have documents concerning the place of origin. Ask family members for old documents, family records, Bibles, or prayer books. Search attics, basements, old trunks, etc., for such items. Often oral traditions and various printed and handwritten

---

*A note of caution: Emigrants from Austro-Hungary usually obtained their passports in the city closest to where the family resided. Often it was required that the applicant and his family report to the police and then remain in the city until the passport was issued. When required later to give their place of origin, some gave the name of this city rather than the actual former residence or birthplace.

Death notices for family and relatives can often give valuable clues about the place of origin of your ancestor as well as information on survivors, relatives who may still be living.

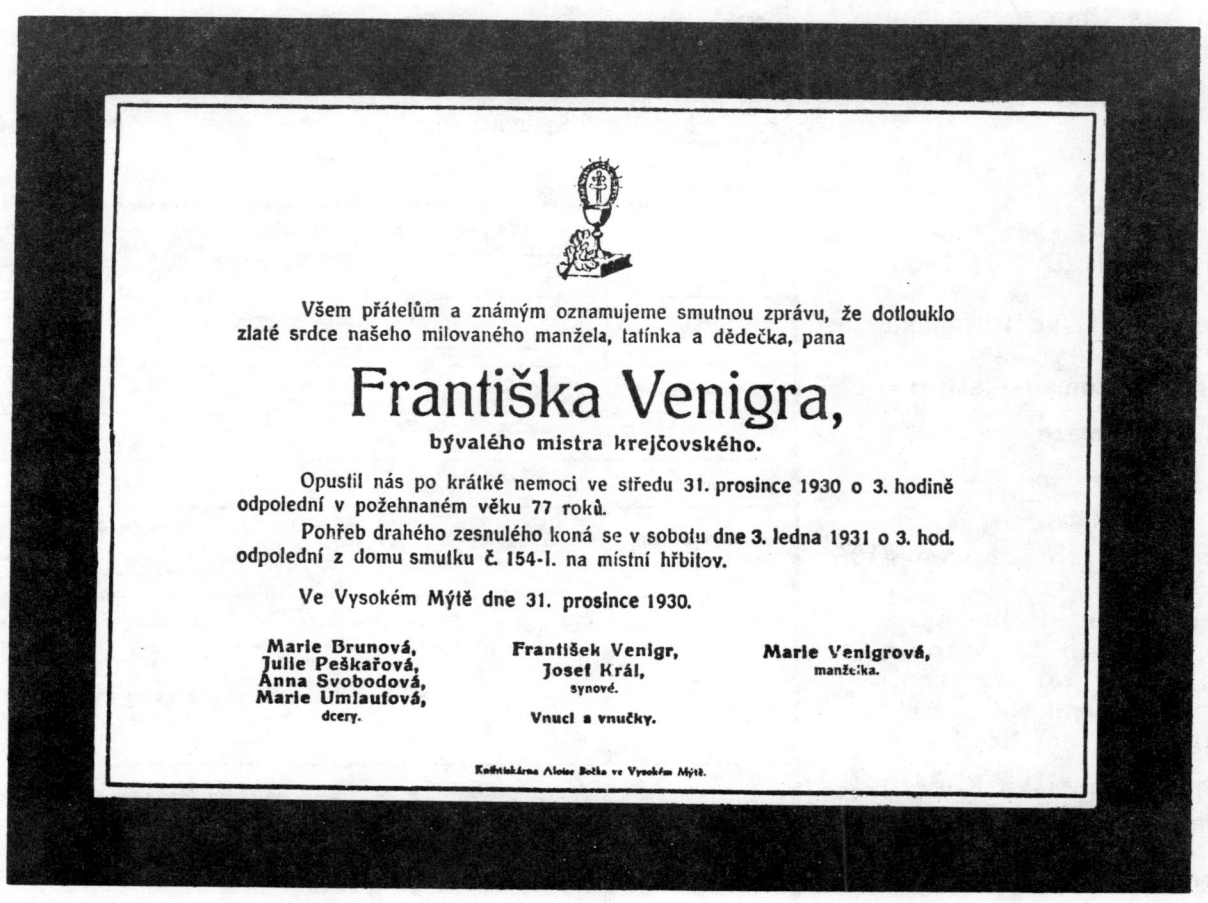

František Venigr
former master tailor

He left us after a brief illness on Wednesday, 31 Dec. 1930, at 3 o'clock in the afternoon, at the blessed age of 77 years.

The funeral of the dearly departed will take place on Saturday, 3 Jan. 1930, at 3 o'clock in the afternoon, from the home of the bereaved, house no. 154-I, to the local cemetery.

In Vysoké Mýto the 31st day of December 1930.

Daughters   Sons   Wife
                      Grandchildren

NO. 6. DEATH NOTICE.

This old birth and christening certificate, issued in 1935, indicates that the place of birth was Choceň, in the district of Vys. Mýto.

Birthdate: 26 Oct 1868
Christening: 27 Oct 1868

Name: Františka Polanská

Religion: Roman-Catholic

Bed: legitimate

Sex: female

Place of birth: Choceň #106

Father: Josef Polanský, farmer, son of Antonín Polanský, tailor, from Prosice, and Kateřina Klatová from Nové Hrady.

Mother: Františka Kučerová, legitimate daughter of Jan Kučera, laborer, from Prosice #37, and Anna Koutná.

Name of Christener: Ignác Lhota.

Godparents: Františka Zavřelová from Sedlice #11.

Midwife: Anna Žižková of Choceň.

NO. 7. BIRTH AND CHRISTENING CERTIFICATE ISSUED 1935.

These certificates were required when traveling to prove place of residence, and they served as a form of identification. Such a certificate sometimes will turn up among old papers belonging to your immigrant ancestor.

Land: Čechy (Bohemia)

Political District: Vysoké Mýto

RESIDENCY CERTIFICATE

for: Lhota Zářec

certifies that

Name: František Houdek

Occupation: worker

Age: born 9 June 1870

Status: single

has right of residency in this town.

Lhota Zářec, day 1 May 1892

Signed by one to whom issued.

František Houdek

Village officials:

Jan Prudič

Václav Prokeš

NO. 8. RESIDENCY CERTIFICATE

materials that appear to be of little value will provide important clues to the place of origin, or perhaps resolve a question about a name change that will open doors for seeking the place of origin in other records.

Many families recorded important family events such as births, baptisms, confirmations, marriages, and deaths on the pages of Bibles, missals, or prayer books, especially those pages next to the front and back covers. Check every page carefully as information may be recorded in the margins. Old photographs should be studied with care. Notations on the back of a photograph may indicate a locality. If the photograph was made in a studio, the name and business address of the photographer may be imprinted. Your ancestor's place of origin likely will not be too far away from the city where the photograph was taken. Old letters may mention family members and places where they lived. Addresses or postmarks on such letters may provide a possible city. Many immigrants brought passports, travel documents, or even birth certificates with them. Others wrote to the old country for birth certificates needed for naturalization, retirement, or other legal matters. These certificates may be preserved and will pinpoint a place of birth. Black-edged death notices of family members in the old country may be found. If a birthplace or other locality is mentioned, it may prove to be your ancestor's place of origin. (See illustrations nos. 6-8.) Old ticket stubs, receipts, or newspaper clippings sometimes can give clues to the place of origin. In any event, such records enrich your background knowledge about the family.

LDS GENEALOGICAL INDEXES

The LDS (Mormon) church has produced several genealogical indexes that can be very helpful to the Czechoslovak genealogical researcher trying to locate his ancestor's place of origin. These records are not for Mormon church members only but are general in scope. LDS indexes include numerous ancestral lines in Czechoslovakia, many of which, with a bit of luck, will tie into lineages of both church members and non-members alike. Since access to genealogical sources in Czechoslovakia has been quite limited until recently, these LDS indexes have not developed into the valuable source that they may become in the future. Nevertheless, a thorough researcher should not ignore them.

A. <u>International Genealogical Index</u>. The LDS source containing the most names is the International Genealogical Index (IGI). The IGI is an index of births and marriages that have been researched and submitted by members of the LDS church. This index, started in 1969, presently encompasses a total of about 86 million names obtained from all over the world. The current edition of this computer file includes approximately 250,000 names from Czechoslovakia. The printout is available on microfiche cards. There are presently seventeen microfiche cards for

K 01								K 01	
REGION: CENTRAL EUROPEAN	COUNTRY: CZECHOSLOVAKIA			AS OF AUG 1981			PAGE 1,434		
NAME	SEX M MALE F FEMALE M HUSBAND W WIFE	T Y P E	EVENT DATE	COUNTY, TOWN, PARISH	B	E	S	SOURCE BATCH	SERIAL SHEET
	FATHER MOTHER OR SPOUSE								
•MROB									
•MROB									
•MROBANOVA, KATERINA	MARTIN BARTOSIK	M M	19MAY1744	HRADISTE UHERSKE,POLESOVICE			24JAN1978PV	7611824	2
•MROBANOVA , •• SEE MROB									
•MROBAR									
MROBAR, BARTOLOMEJ	ANNA VADUROVA	M M	10FEB1778	HRADISTE UHERSKE,POLESOVICE			24JAN1978PV	7611824	2
MROBAR, BERNARD	ROSALIE DVOULETA	M M	19NOV1783	HRADISTE UHERSKE,POLESOVICE			21JAN1975PV	7611824	2
MROBAR, MATHEUS	CATARINA TESAROVA	M M	12JAN1796	HRADISTE UHERSKE,POLESOVICE			21JAN1978PV	7611824	2
MROBAR, TOMASS	KATERINA BURZOVA	M M	08MAY1742	HRADISTE UHERSKE,POLESOVICE			20JAN1978PV	7611824	2
MROBAR, VACLAV	MARINA BARTOSIKOVA	M M	01AUG1753	HRADISTE UHERSKE,POLESOVICE			24AUG1977OG	7611825	2
•MROBSKA									
MROBSKA, TERESIE		F C	10AUG1850	PELHRIMOV,LUKAVEC	CLEARED	CLEARED	CLEARED	8115623	76
CEMEK OR VINCENC MROBSKY/KATERINA NOVAKOVA									
MROBSKA, TERESIE	JAN EVANGELISTA STIBOR	W M	14OCT1873	TABOR,MEZILESI			CLEARED	8115623	77
•MROCH									
MROCH, ANNA	FRANTZ MROCH/	F B	1752	PARDUBICE,KOSTENICE,KOSTENICE	27MAY1977OG	20JUL1977OG	25AUG1977OG	7601623	1
MROCH, ANNA	FRANTISEK MROCH/KATERINA KUCEROVA	F B	10DEC1830	PARDUBICE,KOSTENICE,KOSTENICE	D8APR1977LA	11JUN1977LA	05JUL1977LA	7516743	1
MROCH, BARBORA		F B	07NOV1835	PARDUBICE,KOSTENICE,KOSTENICE	D8APR1977LA	11JUN1977LA	05JUL1977LA	7516743	1
MROCH, FRANTISEK	FRANTISEK MROCH/KATERINA KU OVA	M M	08SEP1680	PARDUBICE,CERADICE			02AUG1977PV	7601626	2
MROCH, JAN	FRANTISEK MROCH/KATERINA KUCEROVA ALZBETA MORAKOVA	M M	30JUL1832	PARDUBICE,KOSTENICE,KOSTENICE	D9APR1977LA	07JUN1977LA	30JUN1977LA	7516743	1
MROCH, JOSEF	FRANTISEK MROCH/MAGDALENA MECHVILOVA	M B	09APR1811	PARDUBICE,KOSTENICE,KOSTENICE	D5MAY1977OG	01JUL1977OG	14OCT1977OG	7601622	1
MROCH, MAGDALENA	FRANTISEK MROCH/KATERINA KUCEROVA	F B	24JUL1848	PARDUBICE,KOSTENICE,KOSTENICE	D8APR1977LA	11JUN1977LA	05JUL1977LA	7516743	1
MROCHOVA, MARENA MAGDALENA	VACLAV VOZENILEK	W M	06JUL1734	PARDUBICE,DASICE			18JUL1967LA	A471939	1293
MROCH, PAVLINA	FRANTISEK MROCH/KATERINA KUCEROVA	F B	29JUL1834	PARDUBICE,KOSTENICE,KOSTENICE	D8APR1977LA	11JUN1977LA	05JUL1977LA	7516743	1
MROCH, VOJTECH	FRANTISEK MROCH/MAGDALENA MECHVILOVA	M B	25MAR1813	PARDUBICE,KOSTENICE,KOSTENICE	D5MAY1977OG	01JUL1977OG	14OCT1977OG	7601622	1
•MROCHOVA , •• SEE MROCH									
•MROMADA									
MROMADKO, ALZBETA		F C	19NOV1833	CHRUDIM,TOPOL	15FEB1960SL	19JUN1980SL	02SEP1980SL	7933922	85

NO. 9. INTERNATIONAL GENEALOGICAL INDEX (IGI).

CZECHOSLOVAKIA that include only names from the Czech lands. Names from Slovakia are included on the microfiche cards for HUNGARY. Each microfiche card has 350 pages of names arranged in alphabetical order (see illustration no. 9). Listed next to the name are the names of the parents, if the entry is from a birth or christening record, or name of the spouse, if it is an extract from a marriage record. In the next column, Sex, the letter F is listed for female, M for male, H for husband, and W for wife. The next column, Event, shows the letter B for birth, C for christening, and M for marriage. The next column indicates the date of the event, and the following column lists the town where the event occurred and its political district or Hungarian county. The last columns are for Source. A batch number is given that can lead you to the source of the information, usually a member of the LDS church who submitted the data. Some data from Czechoslovakia cannot be traced because of sensitive sources. The librarian or branch librarian can provide instructions for finding the input source. Several copies of the IGI are available at the Genealogical Library in Salt Lake City, and copies also are available at most the branch libraries as well. All branch libraries can order a copy, if requested. It should be noted that this printout is updated approximately every two to five years with the addition of several million new names.

 B. Family Group Records Archives. Another LDS source that may be of value to Czechoslovak researchers is the Family Group Records Archives (FGRA) which includes family group sheets submitted by members of the LDS church from 1942 until 1969, when the IGI was initiated. A family group sheet is a form on which genealogical information is recorded for one family consisting of a father, mother, and all known children. Despite the fact that input into this file took place when comparatively little Czechoslovak genealogical research was being attempted, there are a number of sheets for Czechoslovak families.

 C. The Temple Records Index Bureau. The Temple Records Index Bureau (TIB) is a name index file that began in 1921 and ended in 1969. Index cards list the date and place of birth, marriage, and death as well as the names of parents and spouse for each individual submitted. A minuscule number of Czechoslovak names were submitted during this period of time; consequently, this index is of little value to most Czechoslovak researchers. It is mentioned only because it is included on the Temple Ordinance Index Request (TOIR) form. The TOIR form is available at most LDS branch libraries, or may be requested by writing to the Genealogical Library in Salt Lake City. The form provides for a search of the three above-mentioned indexes for a nominal fee.

VITAL RECORDS

 A. Church. Czech and Slovak immigrants usually joined colonies of fellow countrymen whether in large cities or in small agricultural communities. For those whose immigrant ancestors were churchgoers, the church registers of these communities often can provide information on the family and, perhaps, even the place of origin. This is a less likely possibility for Czechs than for Slovaks. Official Austrian statistics indicate that 96% of the population of Bohemia was Catholic; 2.2%, Protestant; 1.6%, Jewish; and only .002% confessing no religion. However, the figures are quite different for American immigrants. Taking Czech residents of New York as an example, only 25% were Catholic; 11%, Protestant; 1.6%, Jewish; and 62% had no church affiliation. These figures, of course, will vary for immigrants from other areas. Many Protestants, for instance, came to this country expressly for the purpose of obtaining freedom to practice their religion. But it can be said that less than half of the Czech immigrants to America remained with their old-country religion. Many found that this new land of religious freedom also extended the right to be apathetic or even bitter toward the religion forced upon them by centuries of Austrian rule.*

For those who remained faithful churchgoers, the christening, marriage, burial, or membership records may indicate the place of origin. Marriage records are particularly good for containing this information. These church records are often preferable to civil (public) vital records because they can be more accurate and complete. Public clerks frequently misspelled the difficult Slavic names or Americanized them.

In order to ascertain which church your ancestor may have attended, you should interview family members and relatives to determine religion, i.e., Roman-Catholic, Greek-Catholic, Lutheran, Brethren, Reformed, Orthodox, etc., then consult a directory to locate the church of that denomination in the place where your ancestor settled. Usually Czechs and Slovaks had their own congregations with services conducted in their own languages. You often can recognize a Czech or Slovak church by the saint after whom it was named. Popular names were St. Wenceslaus, St. Cyril and Methodius, St. Stephen, and St. Vitus. In smaller communities there usually was only one Czech or Slovak church. In larger cities you will need to consult a city map to determine which church was nearest your ancestor's place of residence. Ruthenes from eastern Slovakia and Sub-Carpathian Russia were usually Greek-Catholic, but in this country they may have become Roman-Catholic or Orthodox.

Pastors are usually willing to assist when presented with a request for information but are under no obligation to do so. In many cases the community served by the church has changed

---

*Thomas Capek, Čechs (Bohemians) in America (New York: Houghton Mifflin Co., 1920), p. 119; and Čech Communities in New York (New York: Czechoslovak Section of America's Making, 1921), p. 3.

considerably, so the pastor likely will not be familiar with the language. It is wise, therefore, to make any request as simple as possible. Supply pertinent information with specific dates, etc., and include a donation.

B. <u>Civil</u>. Civil (public) marriage and death records often will provide a place of birth. Birth records may indicate the birthplace of the father and mother. To locate birth, marriage, and death records, consult the booklet <u>Where to Write for Vital Records: Births, Deaths, Marriages, and Divorces</u> by the United States Department of Health and Human Services. This is available at many libraries and from the Superintendent of Documents, GPO, Washington, D.C. 20402 (No. 017-022-00794-1).

CEMETERY RECORDS

Tombstone inscriptions often give clues about the birthplace of the deceased as well as age at death and possible relationships. Other family members and relatives may be buried in nearby plots. However, information from tombstones should be used with caution. The stone may have been erected years after the death by a relative who could only approximate dates, etc. More reliable, but still questionable, are the sexton's records that were made by the cemetery caretaker at the time of burial. Death records of all types are only as reliable as the knowledge of the survivor who supplied the information. Also, some funeral homes keep accurate records and may allow access to them if you clearly explain the purpose of your research.

CENSUS RECORDS

Valuable information can be obtained from the U.S. census records. Since 1790 the United States has taken a census every ten years. As of 1850 the census lists the names and birthplaces (usually only the state or country) for all members of the household. The 1870 census indicates whether or not an individual's parents were foreign born. The 1880 census lists the birthplace (state or country) for each individual as well as for his parents. There is an index (Soundex) to this census for those families with children ten years of age and younger. The 1890 census was destroyed by fire. Both the 1900 and 1910 censuses list age (1900 also gives month and year of birth), state or country of birth, birthplace of parents, date of immigration, how long in the United States, and whether or not naturalized if over age 21. The 1910 census also lists the language spoken. The 1900 census is completely indexed (Soundex); however, the 1910 census has been indexed (Soundex) for only the following 21 states: Alabama, Arkansas, California, Florida, Georgia, Illinois, Kansas, Kentucky, Louisiana, Michigan, Mississippi, Missouri, North Carolina, Ohio, Oklahoma, Pennsylvania, South Carolina, Tennessee, Texas, Virginia, and West Virginia. Census information from 1920 and later is confidential, but information

1880 Census—United States

Dwelling number	Family number	Page	Names	Color	Sex	Age prior to June 1	Month of birth in census year	Relationship to head of house	Single	Married	Widowed	Divorced	Married in census year	Occupation	Other information	Can't read or write	Place of birth	Place of birth of father	Place of birth of mother	Enumeration date

1900 Census—United States

Location			Name of each person whose place of abode on June 1, 1900, was in this family	Relation to head of family	Personal description					Nativity			Citizenship			Occupation		Education			Home owned or rented	Home owned free or mortgaged	Farm or house
Street	House number	Dwelling number	Family number			Color	Sex	Month of birth	Year of birth	Age	Marital status	Number of years married	Mother of how many children	No. of these children living	Place of birth	Place of birth of father	Place of birth of mother	Year of immigration to US	Number of years in US	Naturalization	Occupation	No. of months not employed	Attended sch. (months)	Can read	Can write	Can speak English			

1910 Census—United States

Location				Name of each person whose place of abode on April 15, 1910, was in this family	Relation to head of family	Personal Description							Nativity			Citizenship			Occupation				Education		Property			Veteran of Civil War	Blind or deaf-mute
Street	House number	Dwelling number	Family visit number			Sex	Race	Age	Marital status	Number of years married	Mother of how many children	No. of these children living	Place of birth	Place of birth of father	Place of birth of mother	Year of immigration to US	Naturalized or alien	Language spoken	Occupation	Nature of trade	Employer, worker, or own account	No. of months not employed	Can read and write	Attending school	Owned or rented	Owned free or mortgaged	Farm or house		

NO. 10. UNITED STATES CENSUS RECORDS – FORMAT FOR YEARS 1880, 1900, AND 1910.

can be released about parents and direct-line ancestors. Write to the Bureau of the Census, Pittsburg, Kansas 66762, for Form BC-600, "Application for Search of Census Records." Many states also had censuses that contain information similar to that in federal censuses. These were usually taken at intervals between the federal censuses. Federal census records for 1910 and earlier, as well as many state census records, are on microfilm in the National Archives and its regional branches, the LDS Genealogical Library and a few other genealogical libraries, state archives, and public and university libraries. Your local public library may be able to obtain census films on interlibrary loan. Ask your local librarian about this service.

NATURALIZATION

Although immigrants were not required to become U.S. citizens, your male ancestor very likely filed a declaration of intention and, later, a petition to become a naturalized citizen. The declaration of intention usually was made shortly after arrival in the United States whereas the petition was filed shortly before the naturalization. This required residency in a state for one year and in the United States for five years. These original applications and accompanying affidavits often give the place of birth, country of former allegiance, date of immigration, and the port and date of arrival in the United States. Before 1906, such petitions could be filed at any city, county, state, or federal courthouse, making the petitions difficult to locate. The court that issued the final certificate of citizenship would not necessarily be the same in which the declaration of intention was filed. The actual certificate of naturalization usually lists only the new citizen's name, his native country, and date of naturalization, and is of far less value than the original application. Some immigrants were not naturalized until many years after coming to this country, sometimes as long as 30 or 40 years. For a variety of reasons, many immigrants did not follow through and actually become citizens.

In 1906 the United States established the Bureau of Immigration and Naturalization, and the process of naturalization was standardized. Records after this time are much more complete. The following is a description of information required for the naturalization process after 1906:

DECLARATIONS OF INTENTION: Name, date and port of arrival, occupation, personal description, date and place of birth, citizenship, present address, last foreign address, vessel, and port of embarkation. (Declarations were not necessary if a person entered the country as a minor or was discharged from certain military service.)

PETITIONS FOR CITIZENSHIP: Name, residence, occupation, date and place of birth, citizenship, personal description, date and port of arrival, port of embarkation, marital status, date at which U.S. residence commenced, how long residing in the state, name changes, and names, birthplaces and birth dates of the applicant's spouse and children. After 1930 there often is a photograph.

Naturalization records after 1906 are available from the Immigration and Naturalization Central Office, 425 I Street, N.W., Washington, D.C. 20530; or, you can contact the Immigration and Naturalization office at your nearest federal building and complete Form G-641, "Application for Verification of Information from Immigration and Naturalization Service Records." This verification provides for a search of the master file for the time period 1906 through 1956.

The Genealogical Library has microfilmed some naturalization records of several states. Also, most Federal Record Centers (regional branches of the National Archives) have many naturalization records and some indexes for the areas they serve.

For more details on using naturalization records, refer to <u>Locating Your Immigrant Ancestor, A Guide to Naturalization Records</u>, by James C. and Lila Neagles (Logan, Utah: Everton Publishers, 1975).

Even if your immigrant ancestor never applied for naturalization, there may be another valuable source available through the Immigration and Naturalization Service. Any alien living in the United States after 1940 was required by the Alien Registration Act to register his address each year. The initial registration required specific information that included the date of arrival in the United States, age, and last place of foreign residence. To get information from these records, you must use the same form used for naturalization information.

EUROPEAN PASSENGER LISTS

For Czechs and Slovaks there were three main ports of embarkation: Bremen, Hamburg, and Antwerp. Other significant ports were Rotterdam and LeHavre.

Providing transportation for the emigrants was a highly-competitive business during the second half of the nineteenth century and the early twentieth century. Agents of the numerous shipping companies traveled throughout Europe distributing leaflets and generally promoting their shipping line as the best way to travel at the lowest cost.

The competition between the German ports of Bremen and Hamburg was particularly stiff with each striving for a larger share of passengers. Bremen remained the leader, followed closely by Hamburg, in attracting Austro-Hungarian passengers. Antwerp served as the embarkation point for less than half as

many Austro-Hungarian emigrants as Hamburg. Rotterdam, LeHavre, and other ports took a much smaller share. Available statistics distinguish only between Austrian and Hungarian passengers. Therefore, it is not possible to determine exactly what percentage of Czechs from Austria and Slovaks from Hungary used which port.

Some ports maintained lists of departing passengers that contained information on age, place of origin, and occupation. Passenger lists from Bremen have been destroyed. This is unfortunate since the largest number of Czechs and Slovaks left from this port. Passenger lists for the Port of Hamburg, on the other hand, are still preserved in the German State Archives in Hamburg, and these have been microfilmed by the Genealogical Library. Information on how to use these records is given below. Antwerp port records of passengers exist only for the years 1854-1855, and the available index for those years includes no emigrants from Czechoslovak territory during this time period. The city archives of Antwerp, nevertheless, do have sojourn records for some later years. Sojourn records are lists of travelers who stayed in Antwerp hotels awaiting their departure. These records have not been microfilmed, but the archive may answer specific inquiries or may be able to recommend a researcher. The address of the archive is:

       Stadsarchief Antwerpen
       Venusstraat 11
       2000 Antwerpen
       Belgium

Rotterdam passenger lists have not been maintained, but those of LeHavre are preserved in the departmental archive in Rouen, France. These records hopefully will be filmed by the Genealogical Library in 1985 or 1986.

The Hamburg passenger lists are available for the years 1850 to 1934. In almost every instance, these records list the specific place of last residence or the birthplace for departing passengers. The entire collection is indexed. The indexing is in small segments, each of which covers a year or part of a year. There also is a single alphabetical index for 1856 to 1871, although it is incomplete. A register of microfilm numbers for the passenger lists and complete instructions on their use are given in Research Paper Series C, No. 30, The Hamburg Passenger Lists. This paper is available at many branch libraries. Your branch library may have a newer version entitled Register and Guide to the Hamburg Passenger Lists, 1850-1934. In any event, LDS branch genealogical libraries have a microfiche copy of the Library's locality catalog for Germany. This contains a list of film numbers for the Hamburg passenger lists under the heading **GERMANY, HAMBURG, HAMBURG - EMIGRATION AND IMMIGRATION**.

Because of the segmented nature of the index to the Hamburg passenger lists, you will need to know at least an approximate date of departure from Germany. If your ancestor emigrated between 1856 and 1871, start with the "fifteen-year index" for this period, remembering that this index is incomplete. If your ancestor is not found in this index, or if he did not emigrate during the 1856-1871 time period, you will have to consult other handwritten yearly and part-yearly indexes.

IMPORTANT: The passenger lists are divided into two distinct sections. Be sure to check both sections.

1. The Direct Lists (with Direct Index) for passengers who left Hamburg, Germany, and sailed directly to their designations without stopping at other European ports.

2. The Indirect Lists (with Indirect Index) for passengers who stopped at another European or British port before sailing to their final destination.

After 1910 the sections are combined.

If, for example, one wanted to find the place of origin for Joseph Kubicek of Wisconsin, it would be necessary first to determine the year of immigration. This information usually is given in the 1900 or 1910 U.S. census. The 1900 census lists Josef, age 32, who has been in the United States since 1886.

The second step is to check the indexes to the Hamburg direct passenger lists. If the name is not found in these indexes, check the indexes to the indirect passenger lists. Using the aforementioned microfiche catalog or register, you will find that the direct passenger lists have three indexes for 1886: January to June 1886, July to October 1886, and October 1886 to May 1887. By searching these indexes, an entry for Josef Kubiscek can be located on the third index (see illustration no. 11). This entry indicates that Josef sailed on 10 November 1886 and is found on page 1323 of the actual passenger lists.

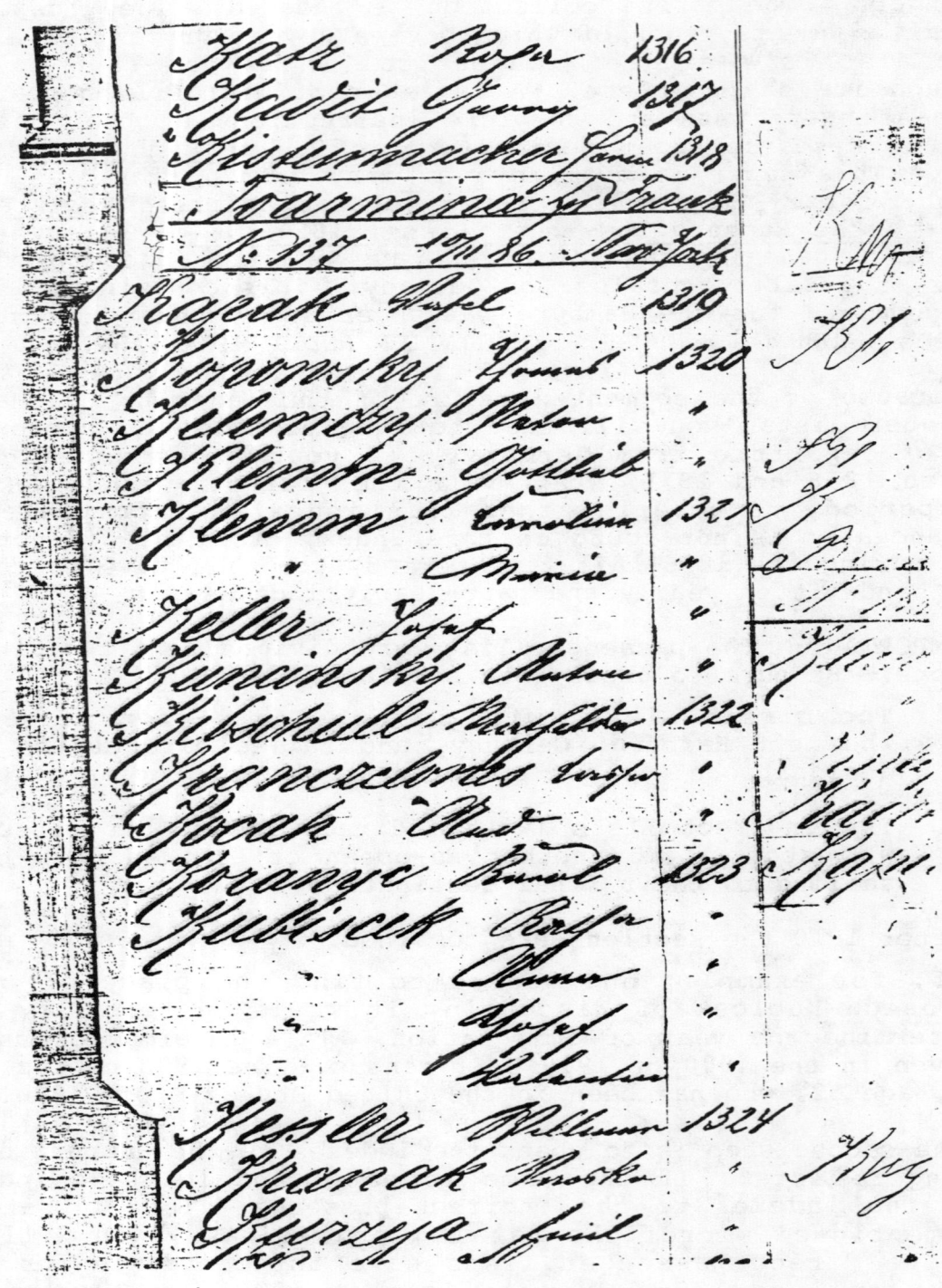

NO. 11. HAMBURG PASSENGER LIST INDEX.

NO. 12. HAMBURG PASSENGER LIST.

The third step is to look at the actual passenger lists. Since Josef was found in the direct indexes, you will want to look at the direct lists. The film numbers for the lists, July to December 1886, are listed in the microfiche catalog or the register. On page 1323 of these lists, Josef Kubiscek, age 17, is listed as coming from Horatev, Bohemia, with his mother (Katherina), sister (Anna), and brother (Valentin) (see illustration no. 12). The age of 17 in 1886 is consistent with the age of 32 in 1900. Other factors, such as family tradition about a sister, Anna, also may confirm that this is indeed the ancestor we want, despite the slight spelling difference.

UNITED STATES PASSENGER LISTS

Records of passenger arrivals in the United States sometimes can prove to be beneficial sources of information. In most cases information given in the passenger arrival records includes the port of departure, port of entry, date of arrival, name of vessel, name, age, sex, occupation, nationality, names of other family members, country or province of origin, and sometimes the specific locality of origin. In most cases, passenger arrival lists prior to the mid 1890s are a poor source for determining place of origin. Most passenger lists give only the country or province of origin. The lists of passengers arriving in American ports from Bremen are a notable exception. Prior to 1870, about 20 percent of the lists of arrivals from Bremen give a specific last residence or birthplace. From 1870 to the late 1880s, the percentage of Bremen arrival lists that give specific place of origin drops sharply. After the late 1880s, Bremen arrival lists again give place of origin in many cases. Thus, although Bremen departure lists are lost, many researchers whose ancestors sailed from this port can find the information they need in the arrival lists. If your ancestors sailed from other European ports, you will not be so fortunate. But you may, nevertheless, benefit from checking the arrival lists.

After 1892 federal law required that immigration passenger lists include last residence, final destination in the United States, and whether the immigrant was going to join relatives in the United States. Unfortunately, this law did not affect New York arrivals until 1897, and other ports did not immediately comply. In June of 1897 passenger arrival registration came under federal administration, and passenger arrival lists became consistent for all U.S. ports. After 1906 the forms used required a personal description and exact birthplace. This does not necessarily mean that the information was always given, but in most cases these later passenger arrival lists are every bit as valuable a research tool as European departure lists.

Most U.S. passenger arrival lists are indexed. The New York lists from 1847 to 1897 are the major exception. These indexes make it a simple matter to find out whether your ancestor arrived at any of the indexed ports, and you can determine if this source will provide a place of origin. The indexes contain errors and are incomplete since the names of some passengers were omitted inadvertently when the indexes were compiled. If your ancestor arrived at New York during the unindexed period, you may want to try alternate research sources before taking on the task of going through the lengthy New York lists. If you are pretty sure your ancestor sailed from Bremen, especially before 1870 or after the late 1880s, you should definitely give the New York lists a try. An inventory of ships from Bremen arriving at New York is available. This inventory indicates which arrival lists show the passengers' specific places of origin and which do not.*

The National Archives in Washington, D.C., has the most complete set of U.S. passenger arrival lists available. If you can determine a fairly exact date of arrival for your ancestor, the port of entry, and the name of the vessel, then the National Archives staff can make a search of the passenger arrival records for you for a fee. To request such a search, use NATF Form 81, "Order for Copies of Ship Passenger Arrival Records," which can be obtained by writing to the following address:

> Reference Services Branch (NNIR)
> National Archives and Records Service
> 8th and Pennsylvania Avenue, NW
> Washington, D.C. 20408

You can search these records yourself, which is not only faster that doing it by mail but also allows a broader scope of research. Lists are available at the National Archives in Washington, D.C., and at its regional branches. At the Genealogical Library and through its branches you also will have access to many of the lists. The Genealogical Library collection includes lists from all major and most minor U.S. ports from 1820 up to World War I. Indexes for all ports, except New York from 1847 to 1897, also are in the Genealogical Library.

SOCIAL SECURITY RECORDS

The Social Security Administration, which was founded in 1934, may be able to help in determining the place of origin

---

*Gary J. Zimmerman, Bremen Arrivals at New York (December 1846-March 1867) (Salt Lake City: photocopy by the Genealogical Society of Utah, 1983), 974.71 W33z, also on microfiche no. 6,010,517. German Immigrants, Lists of Passengers Bound from Bremen to New York, 1847-1854 (pub. 1985) and German Immigrants, Lists of Passengers Bound from Breman to New York, 1855-1862 (pub. 1986), compiled by Gary J. Zimmerman (Baltimore: Genealogical Publishing Company), lists persons arriving at New York from Bremen for whom a specific place of origin is given.

of an ancestor who was still living after 1934 and who had a social security number. Many persons, when making their original application for a social security number, or when making a claim, had to provide proof of age. The proof submitted was often in the form of a birth or christening certificate or other document. This document, which would have been placed in the individual's file, often provides a specific place of birth or origin. You may write for a copy of your ancestor's original application for a social security number if you provide proof of death, social security number (this may be given on the death certificate), relationship, and other facts to aid in positive identification. Genealogy is not a function of the Social Security Administration, so it is best not to make reference to it, but imply a purpose more bureaucratically acceptable. The Social Security Administration may send you a form-letter reply saying that they do not have time to search. Budget cuts have caused an understaffing and consequent backlog of Social Security requests. Third party requests are a low priority, so you may want to indicate the earnestness of your request and willingness to be patient. In recent years it has been increasingly more difficult to get this kind of information, and you may not get a positive response, but it is definitely worth your while to try.

LOCAL NEWSPAPERS AND PERIODICALS

Local newspapers, especially those published in Czech or Slovak, may contain valuable information about your ancestor. Newspapers often reported local births, marriages, and deaths. These announcements may include information about the immigrant's birthplace. Some newspapers periodically published lists of recent immigrants, sometimes with places of origin. The obituaries printed in these newspapers can be extremely valuable. Frequently, the obituary included biographical data, birth date and place, occupation, membership in clubs and societies, and survivors, etc. Often families ran a paid announcement of death or a memorial to the deceased in the newspaper. For some areas obituary indexes have been prepared by local genealogical or historical societies. If an obituary is not available for your ancestor, you may find one for the ancestor's brother, sister, or child who would likely have been born in the same place. Copies of old local newspapers often are found in the local public library. You may need to consult one of the following books:

>Newspapers in Microform, United States 1948-1972. Washington, D.C.: Library of Congress, 1973, plus periodic supplements. (This can be used to determine whether a specific newspaper has been microfilmed and can be ordered on interlibrary loan.)

>Gregory, Winifred. American Newspapers 1821-1936. A Union list of Files Available in the United States and Canada. New York: H. W. Wilson, 1937.

>Jerabek, Esther. Czechs and Slovaks in North America. A Bibliography. New York: Czechoslovak Society of Arts and Sciences in America, 1976. (Pages 314-367 list Czech and Slovak language periodicals and newspapers.)

>Wynar, Lubomyr R., and Anna T. Wynar. Encyclopedic Directory of Ethnic Newspapers and Periodicals in the United States. Littleton, CO: Libraries Unlimited, Inc., 1976. (Pages 63-68 and 174-177 list Czech and Slovak presses.)

Many Czech and Slovak newspapers and periodicals are available in the Slavic and East European collections of the University of Illinois Library, Urbana, Illinois. Also, it is often possible to obtain materials from local and university libraries on interlibrary loan. Ask your local librarian about this service.

Many researchers will be interested in a new magazine for the Czech genealogist. This is Naše Dějiny [Our History] published six times a year by the Old Homestead Publishing Company. The magazine tends to be Texas-Czech oriented but is gradually becoming more universal in its scope. For details about subscribing, write to:

>Naše Dějiny
>Box 45
>Hallettsville, Texas 77964

STATE AND LOCAL HISTORIES

A history of the county or locality where your ancestor settled may include information about your ancestor and any part he may have played in local history. Books of this type often are found in local and county libraries and may be part of the extensive collection of such materials available at the LDS Genealogical Library. An excellent book of this nature for Nebraska is The History of the Czechs (Bohemians) in Nebraska by Rose Rosicky, published originally in 1929. An indexed version is on film no. 1,036,170, item 1, at the Genealogical Library. Often genealogical and historical societies collect histories for their region of interest. The following directories are helpful in locating addresses of these societies: Directory of Historical Societies and Agencies in the United States and Canada, 12th ed., compiled and edited by Tracey Linton Craig (Nashville: American Association for State and Local History, 1982); the American Library Directory, edited by J. C. Press (New York: R. R. Bowker Co., 1982); and the Directory of Special Libraries and Information Centers, by M. L. Young (Detroit: Gale Research Company, 1977).

MILITARY RECORDS

If your ancestor served in a branch of the U.S. military, his service records may provide a place of birth. Military service and pension records and indexes prior to World War I are located in the National Archives. Write to the following address and request NATF Form 80, "Order for Copies of Veterans Records":

> Military Service Branch (NNIR)
> National Archives and Records Service
> 8th and Pennsylvania Avenue, NW
> Washington, D.C. 20408

Upon receipt of a completed NATF Form 80, the staff will search the records for you, and you will be informed of the cost to obtain copies.

All available military service records relating to soldiers who served in World War I and afterwards are available at the address below. Unfortunately, many of these later records were destroyed in a fire in 1973.

> The National Personnel Records Center
> GSA (Military Records)
> 9700 Page Boulevard
> St. Louis, Missouri 63132

You must obtain a questionnaire from the Center and complete it with all possible information to facilitate identification. You also should send copies of any military-related papers you may have pertaining to the ancestor. You must, of course, provide proof of death.

WORLD WAR I DRAFT REGISTRATION RECORDS

For those who had ancestors eligible for the draft in World War I, an excellent source of information recently has become

WORLD WAR I REGISTRATION CARD REQUEST

General Services Administration	National Archives and Records Service

Send this form to: WORLD WAR I REGISTRATION CARD REQUEST   Phone: (404) 763-7477
ARCHIVES BRANCH, FARC
1559 ST. JOSEPH AVENUE
EAST POINT, GEORGIA 30344

On 5 June 1917 all men between the ages of 21 and 31 were required to register for the draft. Those who had turned 21 in the following year had to register on 5 June 1918. A few months later the age categories were extended and, on 12 September 1918, all men ages 18 to 21 and 31 to 45 were required to register also.

More than 24 million World War I Selective Service records are on file at the Center. They are filed by state and by draft board. To search this large file requires the full name of the person and their city and/or county of residence at the time of registration. For the cities listed below, a home street address or other specific location information (such as ward) is required.

Please complete a separate request form for each registration card requested and enclose $5.00 for each. Make checks payable to: NATIONAL ARCHIVES TRUST FUND.

CITIES FOR WHICH A STREET ADDRESS OR OTHER SPECIFIC INFORMATION IS REQUIRED

California
Los Angeles
San Francisco

District of Columbia
Washington

Georgia
Atlanta

Illinois
Chicago

Indiana
Indianapolis

Kentucky
Louisville

Louisiana
New Orleans

Maryland
Baltimore

Massachusetts
Boston

Minnesota
Minneapolis
St. Paul

Missouri
Kansas City
St. Louis

New Jersey
Jersey City
Newark

New York
Albany
Buffalo
New York City
Syracuse

Ohio
Cincinnati
Cleveland

Pennsylvania
Luzerne County
Philadelphia
Pittsburgh

Rhode Island
Providence

Washington
Seattle

Wisconsin
Milwaukee

Registrant Data   (TO BE COMPLETED BY REQUESTOR)

Information about person whose registration card is being requested.

Full Name of Registrant	Birthdate
Home Address at Time of Registration (Street, City, County, and State)	Birthplace (City, County, and State)
Draft Board Location (City, County, Board No.)	Registration Date
Name of Wife or Nearest Relative at Time of Registration	Occupation at Time of Registration

Requestor's Name and Address

Date of Request:

Signature of Requestor

available. On 5 June 1917 all males between the ages 21 and 31 were required to register. In June of 1918 those who had just turned 21 also were required to register. Then in September of 1918 the age categories were extended, and all males from 18 to 45 were required to register. Some aliens did not register but many did, especially young men. In total, some 24 million men registered. The registration card required the registrant to give birth date, birthplace (town, state, country), age, address, occupation, employer, and marital status.

These records eventually may be available through the Genealogical Library, so be sure to check the library catalog. In any event, you may write for a copy of your ancestor's registration card. To request this record, you must know at least the city or county of residence at the time of registration; a specific address is required for larger cities. Additional information is asked for on the application form. Xerox and use the form on page 39. Remember, even though your ancestor may not have registered, a brother or son who was born in the same place may have done so.

OCCUPATIONAL AND FRATERNAL RECORDS

City directories for the town in the United States in which your ancestor lived will sometimes provide information about his occupation. Death records and family traditions may further illuminate the profession or trade of a progenitor. The firm that employed your ancestor, the union, or pension plan to which he belonged also may have kept records. The government required aliens to register with the Department of Labor in order to work. This registration may yield paperwork similar to that shown in illustration no. 14.

Many Czechs and Slovaks joined fraternal benefit societies and social organizations such as SOKOL. Most of these organizations were founded at the end of the nineteenth and beginning of the twentieth centuries. Some of them have maintained their files of fraternal newspapers, board minutes, applications for membership, and, most important, death claims. Most often, however, the records of these firms, societies, unions, insurance companies, etc., have not been preserved; and it may be rather difficult to locate those records that have survived. If the society or firm still exists, try contacting it.

Many fraternal insurance companies that did not preserve the applications have retained books and periodicals. A number of these groups have turned much of their material over to the Czechoslovak Heritage Museum and Library, 2701 South Harlem, Berwyn, Illinois 60402. The museum and library are sponsored by the Czechoslovak Society of America. Founded in 1854, this is the oldest fraternal insurance company in the United States. If you can determine the society to which your ancestor belonged, location of the chapter, and the time period, it may be possible

ORIGINAL No. 18640
File R-21838
FORM NO. 656

**CERTIFICATE OF REGISTRY
U.S. DEPARTMENT OF LABOR
IMMIGRATION SERVICE**

THIS IS TO CERTIFY THAT THE REGISTRY OF ENTRY INTO THE UNITED STATES OF THE ALIEN WHOSE NAME AND DESCRIPTION APPEAR ON THE REVERSE HEREOF HAS BEEN MADE AS PROVIDED IN SECTIONS I AND III OF AN ACT OF CONGRESS APPROVED MARCH 2, 1929.

DATE OF ISSUE January 12, 1931

Harry E. Hull
COMMISSIONER GENERAL OF IMMIGRATION

ORIGINAL

PRESENT NAME: KREHEL (SURNAME) JOHN (FIRST) 39 (AGE)

NAME AT TIME OF ENTRY: Krehel (SURNAME) John (FIRST)

May 1, 1894 (DATE OF ARRIVAL)   New York, New York (PLACE OF ARRIVAL)

Klembark, Eperjes, Czechoslovakia (COUNTRY OF BIRTH)

5 feet 9 inches (PRESENT HEIGHT)   dark (COMPLEXION)   brown (EYES)   black-grey (HAIR)

PLACE OF REGISTRY: Philadelphia, Pennsylvania

DATE OF REGISTRY: January 12, 1931   RECORD OF REGISTRY No. 56796

John Krehel (SIGNATURE OF ALIEN)

Charles B. Richter (SIGNED IN PRESENCE OF)   U.S. IMMIGRANT INSPECTOR (TITLE OF GOVT. OFFICER)

NO. 14. CERTIFICATE OF REGISTRATION FOR AN ALIEN ISSUED BY THE DEPARTMENT OF LABOR.

to find valuable details such as birth date, birthplace, photograph, physical description, and history of the local Czech or Slovak community. The curator, Mrs. Lillian Chorvat, is skilled at using the collection and is happy to assist visitors. She also will help researchers by correspondence. Please remember to make a donation.

PASSPORT APPLICATIONS

If your ancestor traveled abroad, you should check for a passport application. U.S. citizens traveling abroad between 1795 and 1905 may have applied for a passport. Since 1905 all travelers have been required by law to do so. Naturalized citizens before 1906 often submitted naturalization papers with the passport application. The application itself asked for name, signature, place of residence, age, personal description, names or number of other family members intending to travel, date and court of naturalization. Sometimes the applications show exact birth dates and birthplaces of the applicant, spouse, and children; date and port of arrival in the United States; and name of vessel. From 1906 to 1925 the applications include name, date, and place of birth; names, birth dates, and birthplaces of spouse and children; residence, occupation, travel plans, physical description, and photograph.

Applications for 1791 to 1925 are at the National Archives, Record Groups 59 and 84. There is a 75-year restriction on these holdings. For records newer than 75 years, write to the following address:

> Passport Office
> Department of State
> 1425 "K" Street, N.W.
> Washington, D.C. 20520

Bohemian national costumes.

CHAPTER 5

LOCATING THE ANCESTRAL HOME

After you have discovered the name of the town from which your ancestor emigrated, you must still determine its location. Genealogical research in original vital records cannot proceed unless the place of origin has been identified exactly.

Why is this step so important? Many localities have similar names that may be easily confused. An example would be the place names **Kamenec, Kamenica, Kamenice, Kamenka, Kamienka,** and **Kameničany**. Czech grammatical endings can change an actual place name so that the potential for confusion increases. The expression in **Kamenka** is **v Kamence**. Often, many localities are encountered with the same place name. For example, there are nine places called **Kamenice** and one called **Kamenice nad Lipou**.* In addition, there are twelve more places called **Kamenice** preceded by an adjective, such as **Horní Kamenice** [Upper Kamenice], **Česká Kamenice** [Bohemian Kamenice], and **Trhová Kamenice** [Marketplace Kamenice]. There are over 100 places in Czechoslovakia called **Nova Ves**! The names of some places have been spelled several ways, and many places have different names in other languages.

In the Czech lands formerly ruled by Austria, most localities have names in both German and Czech. Some localities in Silesia also may have Polish versions as may some localities in Slovakia. All localities in Slovakia have names in both Slovak and Hungarian, with many places also bearing German names. In the area of Sub-Carpathian Russia, localities had names in Hungarian, Ukrainian, and Slovak. Czechoslovak place names in any language are often mispelled in American sources. Difficult names were shortened and diacritic marks omitted. It is crucial that these problems be resolved before initiating research by correspondence in Czechoslovakia.

---

*Many towns that are located on rivers bear the name of the river as part of the official place name. The term **nad** (sometimes written as n/) means above or on; thus, **Kamenice nad Lipou** means Kamenice on the Lipa river.

GAZETTEERS

There are tools and methods with which you must become familiar in order to identify localities in Czechoslovakia. A gazetteer is a good place to start. A gazetteer, which is defined as a geographical dictionary, is an essential tool for identifying places. These books provide information regarding the correct spelling of place names, variant names, population, political and church jurisdictions, the local economy, religions, languages, ethnic groups, etc. Gazetteers, together with maps and additional details about the locality, often can enable you to identify a specific ancestral point of origin by political district or county. Several important gazetteers are available for Czechoslovakia. There is a general gazetteer for the entire Czechoslovak Republic. Other gazetteers cover more circumscribed areas of the country in greater detail. Following is a discussion of each of these gazetteers with instructions and examples. LDS Genealogical Library microfilm numbers are provided. Some of the gazetteers can be obtained at branch genealogical libraries on microfiche at little or no expense. Check the library catalogs to see if a microfiche version is available.

A. <u>Administratives Gemeindelexikon der Čechoslovakischen Republik</u> [Administrative Gazetteer of the Czechoslovak Republic], issued by das Statistische Staatsamt. Prague: Rudolf M. Rohrer, 1927, 1928 (Ref. 943.7 E5a; Vol. I on film no. 496,719 and Vol. II on film no. 496,720).

This gazetteer gives information on all towns and villages in each area of Czechoslovakia: Bohemia, Moravia (including Austrian Silesia), and Slovakia. In addition, it includes towns in Sub-Carpathian Russia (Podkarpatská Rus), now a part of the Soviet Ukraine Republic, which belonged to Czechoslovakia between the first and second world wars. The gazetteer is arranged by political district with one index for the entire republic. Volume I includes all of Bohemia; Volume II is for the rest of Czechoslovakia.

Main Index:
This index (Vol. II, pp. 257-321) lists all standard Czechoslovak place names, including most German and Hungarian versions. It is alphabetized according to Czech alphabetical order: A B C Č D E F G H Ch I J K L M N O P Q R S Š T U V W X Y Z Ž. (Note that Č, Š, and Ž are alphabetized separately from the unmarked versions, also that Ch comes after H; this means that Sch comes after Sh.)

In some instances, especially in the case of smaller villages, non-Czechoslovak and obsolete names are indexed separately. These additional indexes should be referred to **only** if the locality you are looking for is not found in the main index. These little indexes give the modern (1928) standard version of place names which then can be looked up in the main index.

Following is a list of additional indexes to <u>Administratives Gemeindelexikon</u>.

Czech Name Indexes:
These indexes list the modern Czechoslovak names for old, obsolete names and spellings.
Bohemia (Vol. I, pp. 375-380).
Moravia and Austrian Silesia (Vol. II, pp. 323-325).

Slovak Name Index:
This index (Vol. II, pp. 329-331) lists the modern Czechoslovak names for obsolete Slovak names in Slovakia.

German Name Indexes:
Small villages found only under the Czechoslovak names in the main index are listed by the German names in these indexes.

Bohemia (Vol. I, pp. 381-385).
Moravia and Austrian Silesia (Vol. II, pp. 325-328).
Slovakia (Vol. II, p. 342).
Sub-Carpathian Russia (Vol. II, p. 342).

Hungarian Name Indexes:
These indexes list old Hungarian names detailing the official Czechoslovak names.

Slovakia (Vol. II, pp. 332-342).
Sub-Carpathian Russia (Vol. II, pp. 342-343).

Ruthenian Cyrillic Index:
Ruthenian (Ukrainian) place names (using the Russian Cyrillic alphabet) are listed in Vol. II, pp. 321-322.

Polish Name Index:
This index (Vol. II, p. 328) lists the Czechoslovak names for Polish place names in Moravia and Austrian Silesia.

Use the main index in Volume II to find the locality you want. The index reference gives volume and page number. The figure on the following page is an example of a typical entry from <u>Administratives Gemeindelexikon</u>. Remember that the alphabetical order is not the same as English.

If the source for your place name is from an American document or based on memory, it may be misspelled. Usually the misspelling is phonetic. Study the sounds of the Czech and Slovak alphabets as described in Chapter 8 and try to figure out the likely correct spelling. It also is possible that you have a German or Hungarian spelling, in which case you may need to check a different index, as indicated above; or you may need to use one of the other gazetteers described in this chapter. If there are several localities with the same place name, you should study the section on duplicate place names on page 55.

Administratives Gemeindelexikon is oriented to the German language, with column headings in German. The names of localities are listed in Column 2. In many districts both the Czechoslovak and German versions of place names are listed, with the Czechoslovak version first. Column 3 lists the population according to the census of 1921. Column 4 lists the nationality or language of the village: Czechoslovak (čsl.), German (dtsch.), Hungarian (magy. or maď.), Ruthenian (rus.), Gypsy (zig.) or Jewish (jud.). Mixed nationality is noted and the percentage of Czechoslovaks is given. Column 8 lists the Roman Catholic parish. The parishes for other religions may be mentioned in footnotes or noted in this column as follows: 1. Roman-Catholic, 2. Evangelical Lutheran.

149

Leitmeritz: Lobositz.

Ord.-Zahl	Ortsgemeinde, Ortschaft	Anw. Bevölkerung	Nationalitätschar. d. Gem.	Postamt, Telegraphenamt, Eisenbahntelegraph, E. Telephonamt	Eisenbahnstation, Eisenbahnhaltestelle (H), Eisenb.-Haltestelle u. Ladungspl. (HL)	Volksschule	Pfarramt röm.-kath.*)	Gendarmerieposten	Sanitätsdistrikt
1	2	3	4	5	6	7	8	9	10
	2. G.-B. Lovosice, Lobositz								
1	Boreč, Boretz, 1. ~ ...	349	d.-č. Č.23%	Velemín	(H) Sulejovice; Lovosi-[ce	Sutom d., Vchy-Velemín d. u. č.	[nice č. Sutom Velemín	Lovosice "	Velemín "
	2. Újezd Režný			"	"	"	"	"	"
	3. Bilinka				Lovosice;(H)Sulejovice	"	"	Velemín	"
2	Březno, Priesen	188	d.-č. Č.41%	"	Milešov-Chotiměř; (HL) Oparno	"	"	"	"
3	Čížkovice, Čížkowitz..	986	d.-č. Č.44%	Čížkovice	Čížkovice	Čížkovice d. u. č.	Čížkovice	Čížkovice	Třebenice Osten [sten
4	Děčany	242	čsl.	E Třebivlice	(HL) Semeč; Třebivlice	Solany č.¹)	Třebivlice	Třebivlice	Třebenice We-
5	Děkovka, Diakowa ...	63	č.-d. Č.51%	Třebenice;	(HL) Podsedice	Dlažkovice d., Podsedice č.	Dlažkovice	Třebenice	"
6	Dlažkovice, Dlažkowitz	250	d.-č. Č.45%	E Podsedice	"	Dlažkovice d.u.č.	"	"	"
7	Dobkovice, Dubkowitz	200	dtsch.	Velemín	Dobkovice; Prackovice n. L.; (H) Litochovice	Chotiměř d., Velemín č.	Velemín	Lovosice	Velemín [sten
8	Dřemčice, 1. ~	384	čsl.	E Třebivlice	{ Třebivlice; { (HL) Podsedice	Třebivlice č.	"	Třebivlice	Třebenice We-
	2. Blešno			"		"	"	"	"
9	Chodovlice	355	"	Třebenice	Třebenice	Třebenice d. u. č.	Třebenice	Třebenice	"
10	Chotiměř, Kottomiř...	384	d.-č. Č.26%	Velemín [sedice	Milešov-Chotiměř	Chotiměř d., Velemín č.	Velemín	Lovosice	Velemín [sten
11	Chrášťany	338	čsl.	Třebenice; E Pod-	(HL) Podsedice	Chrášťany č.	Dlažkovice	Třebivlice	Třebenice We-
12	Jenčice, Jenčitz, 1. ~ .	517	d.-č. Č.46%	Třebenice	Třebenice	Třebenice d. u. č.	Třebenice	Třebenice	Třebenice Osten
	2. Košťálov, Kostial .			"	" [Lovosice	"	"	"	" [sten
13	Kocourov, Kotzauer .	71	dtsch.	Milešov p. M.	Milešov-Chotiměř;	Milešov	Milešov	Velemín	"
14	Kololeč	184	č.-d.	Třebenice	Třebenice	Třebenice d. u. č.	Třebenice	Třebenice	Třebenice We-

NO. 15. <u>ADMINISTRATIVES GEMEINDELEXIKON</u> - EXAMPLE OF AN ENTRY.

Politischer Bezirk **Litoměřice, Leitmeritz**

NO. 16. <u>ADMINISTRATIVES GEMEINDELEXIKON</u> - POLITICAL DISTRICT.

A locality may be uniquely identified by the political district in which it is located. The political district is listed in bold type at the top of the page. Because the name of the district at the top of the page often is given in German, it is necessary to check just above the first entry in the district to determine the Czechoslovak version of the district name (see illustration no. 16).

The first entry in illustration no. 15 would be read as follows: Borec (German name Boretz), in the district of Litoměřice, population 349, Germans and Czechs (23% Czech), Roman-Catholic parish of Sutom. The court district (G.-B.) is Lovosice. The locality should be written on genealogical forms Borec, Litoměřice, Czechoslovakia; or, if you want historical accuracy, it may be recorded as Borec, Litoměřice, Bohemia, Austria.*

As a convenience in using this gazetteer, a map of the political districts is on page 60, followed by an index of the districts (pages 61-64). This map shows the relative position of the political districts in Bohemia, Moravia, and Silesia only. It can be very helpful in determining whether towns in different political districts are near each other or far apart. Although the borders of political districts prior to World War I differ slightly, this map still should be quite valuable also in conjunction with the second gazetteer which is described below.

B. <u>Gemeindelexikon der in Reichsrate vertretenen Königreiche und Länder</u> [Gazetteer of the Crownlands and Territories Represented in the Imperial Council], issued by the K. K. Statistischen Zentralkommission (Ref. Q 943.6 E5gk).

   Vol. IX.   <u>Gemeindelexikon von Bömen</u> [Gazetteer of Bohemia], Vienna: Alfred Hölder, 1904 (film no. 1,187,927, item 1). Index, pp. 1135-1311.

   Vol. X.   <u>Gemeindelexikon von Mähren</u> [Gazetteer of Moravia], Vienna: K. K. Hof- und Staatsdruckerei, 1906 (film no. 924,736, item 1). Index, pp. 333-382 and pp. 340-388. Index, pp. 81-91.

   Vol. XI.   <u>Gemeindelexikon von Schlesien</u> [Gazetteer of Silesia], Vienna: K. K. Hof- und Staatsdruckerei, 1906 (film no. 1,187,927, item 2).

---

*In recording genealogical information, it is important always to list the complete names of localities including the diacritic marks. It may seem a nuisance but can prove to be very important. Avoid abbreviations as they often prove to be confusing later on.

District: court district

running number	localities	area in hectares	population			religion				language			institutions there	
			males	females	total	Catholic	Lutheran	Jewish	other	German	Slavic	other	houses	

170

Neutitschein: Fulnek, Neutitschein.

Fortlaufende Nummer	Bezirkshauptmannschaft, Gerichtsbezirk, Ortsgemeinde, Ortschaft	Areal in Hektar	Anwesende Bevölkerung			Konfession				Umgangssprache der einheimischen Bevölkerung			Häuser	Ausstattung mit Institutionen
			männlich	weiblich	zusammen	katholisch	evangelisch	israelitisch	andere	deutsch	böhm., mähr., slovak.	andere		
11	Waltersdorf, Valteřovice	1464	366	402	768	768	.	.	.	768	.	.	124	11. 1) ⌂ I.
1	Groitsch, Gručovice ○		111	114	225	225	.	.	.	225	.	.	38	2) ☦ ⌂ II, ⚒, ⛪, 491 m.
2	Waltersdorf, Valteřovice		255	288	543	543	.	.	.	543	.	.	86	12) ☦, ☦A, Iw. Wintersch., ⌂ VI, ⚒, V 3 ⚒, .
12	Zauchtel, Suchdol	1684	939	1071	2010	920	1056	34	.	1924	48	12	227	3 A, ⛪, 2 ⌂, 2 ℂ, 2 ⛪ (Nordbahn 250 m. Lokalbahn 248 m). Iw
	Summe des Gerichtsbezirkes Fulnek	12160	6325	7082	13407	12218	1102	87	.	13120	143	58	1802	Bezirksverein, 280 m.
	III. Gerichtsbezirk Neutitschein, Jičín Nový 32 ⊕, 2 ⊚, 1 ⊙													1) ♂, ⌂ IV, Versorgungsanstalt, ⚒, 2 ⚒, ⛪, ⌂ 486 m. ca. 395 m.
1	Alttitschein, Jičín Starý	347	321	336	657	656	.	.	1	5	651	.	93	2) ♂, ⌂ II, ⚒, ⛪, (Kunewald)
2	Barnsdorf, Bernatice	938	401	431	832	832	.	.	.	19	813	.	115	246 m, ca. 300 m.
3	Blattendorf, Blahutovice	599	185	216	401	400	1	.	.	389	10	1	59	3) ⌂ I, ⛪. 4) ⌂ II, Versorgungsanstalt, ⚒, ⛪, ⛪,
4	Blauendorf, Bludovice ○	522	276	333	609	601	8	.	.	.	562	39	.	73	299 m. 5) ♂, ⌂ IV, ⚒, ⛪, 2 ⚒,
5	Deutsch Jaßnik, Jasenice	1070	582	633	1215	1205	2	8	.	1213	.	.	170	2 ⛪, ⛪ 262 m, 270 m.
6	Ehrenberg, Loučka	649	398	410	808	797	11	.	.	42	759	4	97	6) ⌂ II, ⚒, ⛪. 7) ☦, ⌂ III, ⚒, ⛪, 284 m.
7	Grafendorf, Hrabětice ○	440	39	48	87	87	.	.	.	87	.	.	17	9) ⌂ I.
8	Großpetersdorf, Vračno, auch Vražné	535	236	277	513	513	.	.	.	511	.	.	87	10) † 269 m, ⌂ II, ⚒, 11) ⌂ II, ⛪, ⛪, ⛪, (Hotzendorf) 391 m.
9	Halbendorf, Poloves ○	342	156	161	317	317	.	.	.	317	.	.	62	12) ♂, ☦A, 2 ⌂ III, ⚒,
10	Hausdorf, Hukavice	498	284	348	632	628	.	4	.	632	.	.	96	2 ⚒, ⛪, 2 ⛪, (Stranik-Hotzendorf) 327 m, 342 m.
11	Hostaschowitz, Hostašovice	928	254	305	559	557	1	1	.	14	544	.	81	14) ⌂ I. 15) ⌂ I, ⚒. 16) ⌂ I, 3 A, ⚒, ⛪.
12	Hotzendorf, Hodslavice ○	1103	777	905	1682	550	1132	.	.	.	1661	.	202	18) ♂, ⌂ V, 2 ⚒, ⛪, ⛪, 250 m. 19) ♂, ⌂ III, ⚒, ⛪, 297 m.
13	Hurka, Hůrka	441	145	148	293	293	.	.	.	.	293	.	45	20) ♂, ev. Filialgemeinde A. K., 2 ⌂ IV, ⚒, ⛪,
14	Itschina, Jičina ○	326	184	210	394	393	1	.	.	.	394	.	58	⛪, ⛪, 358 m, 357 m.
15	Janowitz, Janovice ○	336	121	149	270	270	.	.	.	.	270	.	51	21) Bezirkshauptmannschaft, Baubezirksleitung, Bezirkssanitätsrat, Bezirksschulrat, Bezirkskrankenkasse, Hauptsteueramt, Hauptzollamt I, Grundsteuerkatasterevidenzhaltung, Finanzwachkontrollbezirksleitung, ⛪, Tabakhauptfabrik, ⌂, Kreisgericht, Landesbesserungsanstalt, Bezirksgericht, 2 Notare, 6 Adv., Dek., †, Elisabethinerinnen, Borromäerinnen, ev. Filialgemeinde A. K., Realschule, lw. Mittel
16	Katzendorf, Lhota, auch Kočlčí Lhota ○	554	170	194	364	362	2	.	.	.	364	.	58	
17	Kojetein, Kojetín	267	100	106	206	206	.	.	.	.	206	.	35	
18	Kunewald, Kunvald	1732	1014	1102	2116	1973	130	13	.	2082	18	8	256	
19	Liebisch, Libhošť ○	769	656	717	1373	1373	.	.	.	5	1361	.	199	
20	Murk, Mořkov ○	1085	738	859	1597	1184	413	.	.	.	1597	.	250	
21	Neutitschein, Jičín Nový ⊚	558	5559	6444	12003	11560	186	253	4	10654	1088	53	919	
	darunter Militär				1	1	.	.	.	1	.	.		

schule, Fachsch. für Weberei, kaufm. Fortbsch., gw. Fortbsch., Fortbsch. für Mädchen, 2 Bach. VI, 2 ⌂ XX, Arbeitsch, französische Sprachsch., 2 Musiksch., Stenographiesch., 2 A, städt. Volksbücherei, städt. Museum, allg. ⌂, 3 Versorgungsanstalten, Waisenhaus, Krippe, 2 Apotheken, 7 ⚒, 2 ⛪, ✠ 7 ⚒, 2 ⛪, ⛪, 6 A, Nebenstelle der Öst.-ung. Bank, ⛪, 2 ⛪, Pfandleihanstalt, kr. ⛪, ⛪, ⛪, 2 ⛪ (Nordbahn 283 m, Lokalbahn 270 m), ⛪, 2 lw. Bezirksvereine (d. u. b.), 285 m.

Ortsbestandteile ad Gerichtsbezirk Fulnek:
11. 2) Waltersdorf, Valteřovice ○ 85—589, & ⛪ 1—4.
12. —) Zauchtel, Suchdol ⊙ 215—1923, & ⛪ 12—87.

NO. 17A. GEMEINDELEXIKON VON MÄHREN - LEFT-HAND PAGE.

District: court district

corresp. number	Taxation Area	taxation information — area in hectares									livestock			
		Total	Taxable	Farmland	Meadow	Gardens	Vineyards	Pasture	Woods	Estate land	Industry	Horses	Cows	Sheep	Swine

Neutitschein: Fulnek, Neutitschein.

Nr. der Ortsgemeinde	Bezirkshauptmannschaft, Steuerbezirk, Katastralgemeinde	im ganzen	steuerpflichtige Flächen	Äcker	Wiesen	Gärten	Weingärten	Hutweiden	Wald	Großgrundbesitzungen	Fabriken	Pferde	Rinder	Schafe	Schweine
11	Groitsch, Gručovice (1)	407	399	240	40	7·61	.	13	98	1	.	.	.	.	.
	Waltersdorf, Valtéřovice (2)	1057	1034	614	92	20	.	26	282	.	.	86	866	81	250
12	Zauchtel, Suchdol	1684	1633	1142	280	44	.	10	157	23	.	168	1176	.	684
	Summe des Steuerbezirkes Fulnek	12160	11823	8015	1285	291	.	275	1957	47	.	1201	7660	106	2560

III. Steuerbezirk Neutitschein, Jičín Nový 34 □

1	Alttitschein, Jičín Starý	347	335	222	28	9·47	.	5·29	76	1	.	13	107	.	57
2	Barnsdorf, Bernatice	938	904	599	156	25	.	20	104	1	.	89	695	.	232
3	Blattendorf, Blahutovice	599	585	428	54	15	.	14	74	2	.	41	360	.	303
4	Blauendorf, Bludovice	522	505	298	44	20	.	52	91	.	.	60	296	2	78
5	Deutsch Jaßnik, Jasenice	1070	1035	827	154	26	.	12	16	1	1	86	792	.	297
6	Ehrenberg, Loučka	649	627	400	73	23	.	34	97	1	1	90	448	21	57
7	Grafendorf, Hrabětice	440	438	188	17	2·88	.	5·11	275	1	.	2	95	.	29
8	Großpetersdorf, Vračno	535	519	421	65	21	.	10	1·84	.	.	44	406	.	224
9	Halbendorf, Polouves	342	332	225	59	16	.	4·77	27	2	.	20	274	.	104
10	Hausdorf, Hukavice	498	482	377	78	6·32	.	14	6·71	1	.	61	386	.	97
11	Hostaschowitz, Hostašovice	928	911	238	49	7·38	.	13	604	1	.	32	245	1	101
12	Hotzendorf, Hodslavice	1103	1069	519	127	21	.	41	358	1	.	64	600	.	259
13	Hurka, Hůrka	441	427	256	41	8·27	.	10	112	.	.	44	240	15	140
14	Itschina, Jičina	326	312	192	24	14	.	42	40	.	.	27	230	1	72
15	Janowitz, Janovice	336	327	288	25	5·46	.	11	48	1	.	37	232	.	85
16	Katzendorf, Lhota	554	536	356	56	8·24	.	7·89	108	1	.	40	262	.	102
17	Kojetein, Kojetín	267	259	125	11	5·01	.	28	90	.	.	18	167	.	38
18	Kunewald, Kunvald	1732	1664	1197	245	85	.	40	97	11	2	272	1259	.	369
19	Liebisch, Libhošť	769	746	529	100	29	.	43	45	1	.	52	436	.	82
20	Murk, Mořkov	1085	1049	413	147	15	.	59	415	1	.	51	516	1	83
21	Neutitschein Stadt, Jičín Nový Město (158–2472)	8	1	.	.	0·69	.	.	.	.	.	.	.	.	.
	Neutitschein Obere Vorstadt, Jičín Nový Horní Předměstí (415–5140)	226	188	134	16	32	.	6·27	.	2	31	.	.	.	.
	Neutitschein Untere Vorstadt, Jičín Nový Dolní Předměstí (346–4391)	324	290	252	17	16	.	5·14	.	1	.	189	113	3	57

Ortsbestandteile ad Gerichtsbezirk Neutitschein:

1, —) Alttitschein, Jičín Starý ⊙ 92–650, Palacka Keř ⚭ 1–7.
2, —) Barnsdorf, Bernatice ⊙ 114–819, Waldmühle, Lesní Mlýn ☼ 1–13.
3, —) Blattendorf, Blahutovice ⊙ 58–393, Blattendorfer Mühle, Blahutovický Mlýn ☼ 1–8.
5, —) Deutsch Jaßnik, Jasenice ⊙ 169–1165, Untere Mühle, Dolní Mlýn ☼ 1–50.
6, —) Ehrenberg, Loučka ⊙ 95–759, Pochet, Pocheta △ 2–49.
8, —) Emaus, Emouzy ⚭ 1–5, Großpetersdorf, Vračno ⊙ 86–508.
10, —) Hausdorf, Hukavice ⊙ 94–625, Lapatsch, Lapač ⚭ 2–7.
11, —) Domoratz, Domorac △ 7–55, Hostaschowitz, Hostašovice ⊙ 74–504.
13, —) Hurka, Hůrka ⊙ 44–288, Hurker Hof, Hůrecký Dvůr ⚭ 1–5.
17, —) Kojetein, Kojetín ⊙ 34–201, Teufelsmühle, Čerták ☼ 1–5.
18, —) Barwighäusel ⚭ 1–10, Kunewald, Kunvald ⊙ 255–2106.

NO. 17B. GEMEINDELEXIKON VON MÄHREN – RIGHT-HAND PAGE.

This series of gazetteers is based on the 1900 Austrian census. The gazetteer for each province is organized by political district with an index to both German and Czech place names according to the standard English alphabetical order. Volume X, for Moravia, is a bilingual gazetteer with separate sections, each with its own index; the first section is in German, the second in Czech.

Using Ehrenberg in Moravia as an example, the index to Volume X refers the user to page 170, which is reproduced here on pages 48-49. This gazetteer is arranged with information continuing across two pages. The left-hand page includes population and religion figures. Notice that the page includes footnotes. Often the index will refer to localities too small to appear in the main place-name column; these areas may be so small as to appear only in the footnotes as hamlets subordinate to larger villages or towns.

The German version of the place name is given first followed by the Czech version. The entry shown indicates that Ehrenberg also is known by the Czech spelling Loučka. It is in the district of Neutitschein (the district name is given in German). For the Czech version of the district name, one must see the entry for the city of Neutitschein (Czech: Jičín Nový).* The court district [Gerichtsbezirk] also is Neutitschein (Jičín Nový). The total population of Loučka is 808, of whom 11 are Evangelical Lutherans. The population is almost entirely Czech-speaking, with only 42 German-speaking and 4 others. On the right-hand page, information on land use and livestock is given.

The parish is not noted in the main text but is listed in an appendix, located between the main gazetteer and index of each volume. The appendix has political districts in alphabetical order, each divided into court districts as in the main gazetteer. The parish is given in the last column (see illustration no. 18). For Ehrenberg the Roman-Catholic parish was in Alttitschein (Czech: Jičín Starý).

C. <u>Magyarország Helységnévtára</u> [Gazetteer of Hungary] by János Dvorzsák, comp. Budapest: "Havi Füzetek," 1877 (Ref. 943.9 E5d; Vol. I, Index, on film no. 599,564, and Vol. II on film no. 973,041).

The areas of Slovakia and Sub-Carpathian Russia were formerly part of the Kingdom of Hungary. This gazetteer can provide valuable information about the Hungarian standard spelling, political

---

*This gazetteer, like <u>Administratives Gemeindelexikon</u>, usually turns Czech place names backwards. This properly should be Nový Jičín, meaning New Jicin. The part of the place name ending in -á, -é, -í, or -ý usually should be in first position.

310

Neutitschein: Neutitschein. — **Nikolsburg:** Nikolsburg.

Bezirkshauptmannschaften, Gerichtsbezirke, Ortsgemeinden	Standorte der Schulen,	Sanitätsgemeinden, bezw. Sanitätsdistrikte,	Standorte der röm.-kath. Matrikelstellen,
	zu welchen die nebenstehenden Ortsgemeinden gehören		
III. GB. **Neutitschein**	School	Sanitation District	Parish
Alttitschein	Alttitschein	Alttitschein	Alttitschein
Barnsdorf	Barnsdorf	Alttitschein	Barnsdorf
Blattendorf	Blattendorf	Deutsch Jaßnik	Deutsch Jaßnik
Blauendorf	Blauendorf	Söhle	Neutitschein
➤ Deutsch Jaßnik	Deutsch Jaßnik	Deutsch Jaßnik	Deutsch Jaßnik
Ehrenberg	Ehrenberg	Alttitschein	➤ Alttitschein
Grafendorf	Deutsch Jaßnik	Deutsch Jaßnik	Deutsch Jaßnik
Großpetersdorf	Großpetersdorf	Deutsch Jaßnik	Großpetersdorf
Halbendorf	Halbendorf	Deutsch Jaßnik	Deutsch Jaßnik
Hausdorf	Hausdorf	Nesselsdorf	Partschendorf
Hostaschowitz	Hostaschowitz	Hotzendorf	Hotzendorf
Hotzendorf	Hotzendorf: 2 🕮	Hotzendorf	Hotzendorf
Hurka	Hurka	Alttitschein	Alttitschein
Itschina	Alttitschein	Alttitschein	Alttitschein

NO. 18. GEMEINDELEXIKON VON MÄHREN - POLITICAL DISTRICT.

jurisdiction, and the location of the parish or synagogue. The Genealogical Library uses this gazetteer as the standard for cataloging materials for this area of Czechoslovakia.

Example: Peter Semanček appears on the Hamburg passenger lists, discussed in Chapter 4 (see illustration no. 12, p. 33), as passenger 165 from Gocs, Ung. (Ung. = Ungarn, the German word for Hungary).

Volume I (film no. 599,564) lists all place names in alphabetical order: A B C D E F G H I J K L M N O Ö P Q R S T U Ü V W Y Z. The long vowels, those with a length mark (á, ű, etc.), are assimilated with the short vowels. This volume includes all versions of place names, including German and Slavic names. Many place names are followed by an equal sign (=) which means "see." This refers you to another version of the place name. Other entries are followed by a bow (⌒); this indicates a small farmstead (puszta), settlement (telep) or mill (malom) and refers you to the larger community to which it belongs. Entries in the index are followed by the name of the old Hungarian county (Megye in Hungarian, Comitat in German), and a set of numbers. The first number is the sequential number of the county; the second is the consecutive number of the district (járás in Hungarian, bezirk in German); the last is the number of the locality. These numbers refer to the gazetteer entry in Volume II. The numbers are followed by the name of the post office or, if the village had its own post office, by a horn.

For Gócs the following is listed: Gócs, Gömör 20, 2, 13, Alsó Sajó. This means that Gócs is in Gömör county. In Volume II this is the 20th county, Gócs is in the 2nd district, the 13th town listed, and the post office is Alsó Sajó.

For further details, refer to Volume II (film no. 973,041). This volume is arranged by counties and districts. Counties are numbered at the heads of the pages. The 20th county will be located by the heading **20, Megye - Comitat: Gömör**. Then look for the 2nd district, indicated by **2, Jaras - Bezirk: Rozsnyo**. The 13th town listed in this district is Gócs.

> 11. **Geczelfala** (Gecelfalva, Getzefalva, Gecelfalu), rk. 14 Csetnek, **ÁG. 242 Tiszai**, ref. 1 —, izr. 2 —.
> 12. **Genes** (Genesaiu), rk. 55 Csetnek, ág. 326 Csetnek, izr. 3 —.
> 13. **Gócs** (Gocsova), rk. 32 Dobsina, kg. 2 —, ág. 436 Oláhpatak, ref. 7 —.
> 14. **Hankova**, rk. 9 Csetnek, ág. 229 F.-Sajó, izr. 4 —.

Additional names by which the locality is known are listed in parentheses; the names of subordinate farmsteads (p. puszta), settlements (t. telep), and mills (m. malom) are sometimes listed within brackets. Population figures then follow according to religion. The following abbreviations are used:

```
rk.  - Római Katholikus  - Roman Catholic
gk.  - Görög Katholikus  - Greek Catholic
kg.  - Keleti Görög      - Greek Orthodox
ág.  - Ágostai           - Augsburg Evangelical Lutheran
ref. - Református        - Reformed
un.  - Unitarius         - Unitarian
izr. - Izraelita         - Jewish
```

If the village had its own parish church (or Jewish synagogue), the abbreviation for the religion will be in boldface capital letters followed by the diocese, also in bold type. The abbreviation in lower case means that the people attended church elsewhere, and the population figure is followed by the name of the parish location. If a dash ( ) follows the population figure, it means members of that religion belong to no particular parish.

The entry for Gócs would be read as follows: also known as Gocsova, 32 Roman-Catholic inhabitants belonging to the parish at Dobsina, 2 Orthodox inhabitants with no parish, 436 Lutheran inhabitants belonging to the parish at Oláhpatak, and 7 Reformed inhabitants with no particular parish. Geczelfalva, number 11, had its own Evangelical-Lutheran parish church belonging to the diocese of Tiszai, as indicated by the bold type.

D. <u>Názvy obcí na Slovensku za ostatných dvesto rokov</u> [Place Names in Slovakia During the Last 200 Years] by Milan Majtán. Bratislava: Slovenska Akademie Vied, 1972 (Ref. 943.73 E2m, on film no. 1,181,569, item 1).

This is an excellent gazetteer for Slovakia. The index (pp. 487-667) lists localities by all alternate versions in

Slovak, Czech, Hungarian, German, Russian, Polish, and obsolete Slovak. Standard modern Slovak place names are not in the index; these are arranged alphabetically as the text of the book. Adjectives do not affect the alphabetical order in the text. Thus, Vel'ke Chievany is alphabetized with the Chs after the Hs. Use this gazetteer to determine the modern (1972) standard spelling for any locality in Slovakia, or you can use it to find the Hungarian version of a Slovak place name to facilitate using Magyarország Helségnévtára, explained on pages 50-52.

Example: If Peter Semančcek of Gócs was of the evangelical religion, you will need to use the modern version of the parish, Oláhpatak, when corresponding for research purposes. In the index can be found: Oláhpatak 2907. This means entry number 2907.

2907
VLACHOVO Ro (gemer.)
  1773 Olah-Pataka, Vlachowetz, Wlachowecz, K 1786 Olah-Pataka, Wlachowecz, L 1808 Oláhpataka, Lambsdorf, Wlachow, 1863 Olápatak, 1873–1913 Oláhpatak, 1920 Vlachovo, Vlachov, 1927– Vlachovo

The modern standard Slovak name is given next to the entry number: Vlachovo. This is followed by an abbreviation for the modern Slovak political district and, in parentheses, the old Hungarian county (gemer.). This is the Slovak abbreviation for Gömör County.

The text of the entry gives other names by which the locality has been known over the last 200 years. The village was known in 1773 by the Hungarian name **Olah-Pataka** and the Slavic name **Vlachowetz** or **Wlachowecz**. In 1808 it was known by the German name **Lambsdorf**. From 1873 to 1913, when Peter Semančcek attended the parish there, it was called **Oláhpatak**.

Some entries indicate that a village was merged with another. For example, entry 2908 indicates that village A, **Krmeš**, has merged with **Vlachy**.

2908 – A
VLACHY LM (liptov.)
  1773 Nagy-Olaszj, Wlachy, K 1786 Nagy-Olaszi, Welké Wlahi, L 1808 Nagy-Olaszi, Welké Wlachy, 1863–1913 Nagyolaszi, 1920– Vlachy
  A 1773 Körmes, Krmež, K 1786 Körmesch, Krmesch, L 1808 Körmes, Kermeš, Krmeš, 1863 Körmösháza, 1873–1913 Körmös, 1920–1924 Krmeš

SLOVAK ABBREVIATIONS FOR HISTORICAL HUNGARIAN COUNTIES
(See Map of Historic Hungarian Counties on page 59.)

(abov.)	Abauj-Torna	(ostrihom.)	Esztergom
(bratisl.)	Pozsony	(ráb.)	Győr
(gemer.)	Gömör	(spiš.)	Szepes
(hont.)	Hont	(šariš.)	Sáros
(komárn.)	Komárom	(tekov.)	Bars
(liptov.)	Liptó	(trenč.)	Trencsén
(mošon.)	Moson	(turc.)	Turóc
(nitr.)	Nyitra	(užhorod.)	Ung
(novohrad.)	Nógrád	(zemplín.)	Zemplén
(orav.)	Árva	(zvolen.)	Zolyom

A list of abbreviations for the modern Slovak political districts is given on the flyleaf at the beginning of the book and on the microfilm and microfiche.

E. <u>Other Gazetteers</u>.

1. <u>Orientierungs Lexikon der Tschechoslowakischen Republic</u> [Informational Dictionary of the Czechoslovak Republic] by Ernst Pfohl. Liberec: Gebrüder Stiepel, 1931 (Ref. Q 943.7 E5p, on film no. 928,610). All localities are in English alphabetical order. This gazetteer translates place names but gives the political district and all other data in German.

2. <u>Seznam míst v království Českém</u> [List of Localities in the Kingdom of Bohemia]. Prague: Mistrodržitelské knihtiskárny, 1893 (943.71 E5o, film no. 1,184,071, item 4). This gazetteer has two separate indexes at the end, one in Czech and one in German. All entries are given in both languages. The German text is written in Gothic type.

3. <u>Místní jmena v Čechách</u> [Place Names in Bohemia], 5 volumes, by Antonin Profous and Jan Svoboda. Prague: Nakladatelství československé akademie věd, 1949-1960 (943.71 E2p, film no. 1,181,602). This gazetteer lists all localities in Bohemia in alphabetical order, explains the origin of the name and meaning, and lists any name changes. Volume 5 is an addenda.

4. <u>Místní jmena na Moravě a ve Slezsku</u> [Place Names in Moravia and Silesia], Vol. I, A-L, Vol. II, M-Z, by L. Hosak and R. Sramek. Praha: Nakladatelství československé akademie věd, 1970, 1980 (943.72 E2hs, film no. 1,183,539, item 4). This gazetteer lists all localities in Moravia and Silesia in alphabetical order; explains origin of place names, meaning, and changes in the name of the locality.

F. **Duplicate Place Names.**

In some cases these gazetteers will list several places with the name you are seeking. If this occurs there are several ways by which you can determine the location of your ancestral home.

First, review what you know about your ancestor's place of origin. Was it large or small? Was the population predominantly German? Czech? Slovak? Hungarian? Did the place have a substantial number of Protestants? Jews? Or was it entirely Roman-Catholic? Do you know the province, district, or other jurisdiction? Do you know the name of any nearby city or town?

Second, look up each of the several localities and see if the gazetteers give information that makes some localities better candidates and eliminates others. If, for example, you know your ancestor was from Bohemia, you can eliminate any localities of the same name in Moravia or Slovakia. If your ancestor was Jewish, you can eliminate any localities that had no Jewish population. If one of the several localities is near or in the same district as another locality you know relates to your family, then this would help confirm it as the correct place of origin. You also may use maps to determine which place is correct. Family information may indicate that the ancestral home was on a river or lake, near a border, or in a mountainous area.

MAPS

Often it is necessary to use both a map and a gazetteer to determine exactly from which locality your ancestor came.

Detailed maps (1:75,000) of the former Austro-Hungarian Empire are available on microfilm no. 1,045,395. This, of course, includes all of Czechoslovakia. Place names on these maps will be mostly in German and Hungarian, with some in Czech and Slovak. It should be noted that these maps were prepared shortly before World War I, and many localities in Hungary changed their Hungarian names to completely different Hungarian names between the time of the Hungarian gazetteer (1877) and the preparation of these maps. To use the maps, one must first know the general area of Austro-Hungary needed in order to locate the appropriate map section. The first part of the film has a map grid overview [Übersichtsblatt] of the entire empire, from which the selection of a specific map must be made. A reduced version of this overview, with the modern borders of Czechoslovakia added, is on page 56.

The overview for the Austro-Hungarian map is marked off into grids with bold lines. Each grid is divided into quarters designated by a prominent town. Each of the bold squares has a map number (see illustration no. 20). If a map number is

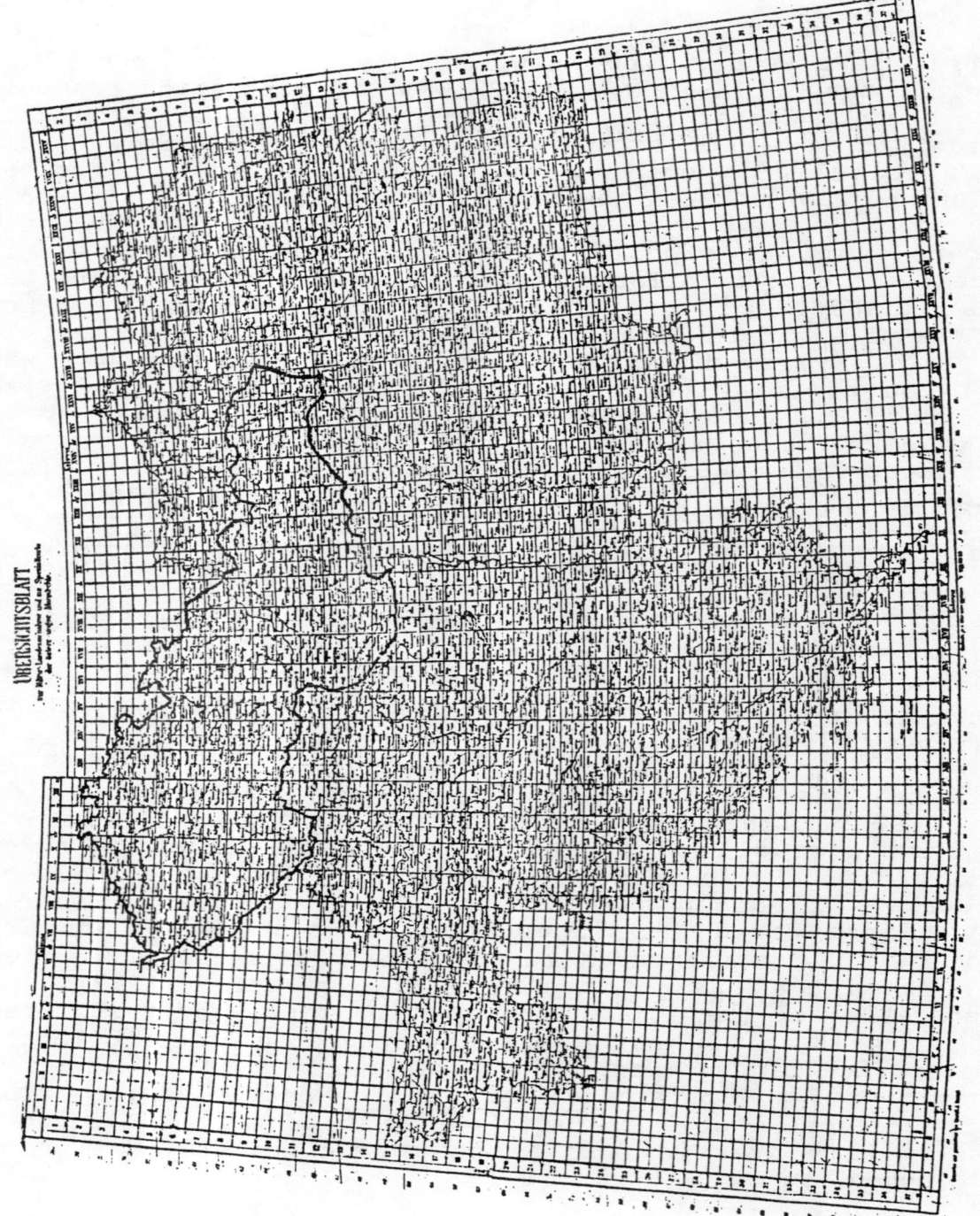

NO. 19. MAP GRID OVERVIEW (1:75,000) - AUSTRO-HUNGARIAN EMPIRE.

difficult to read, it can be determined by comparing it with adjacent grid squares. The maps are filmed in numerical order.

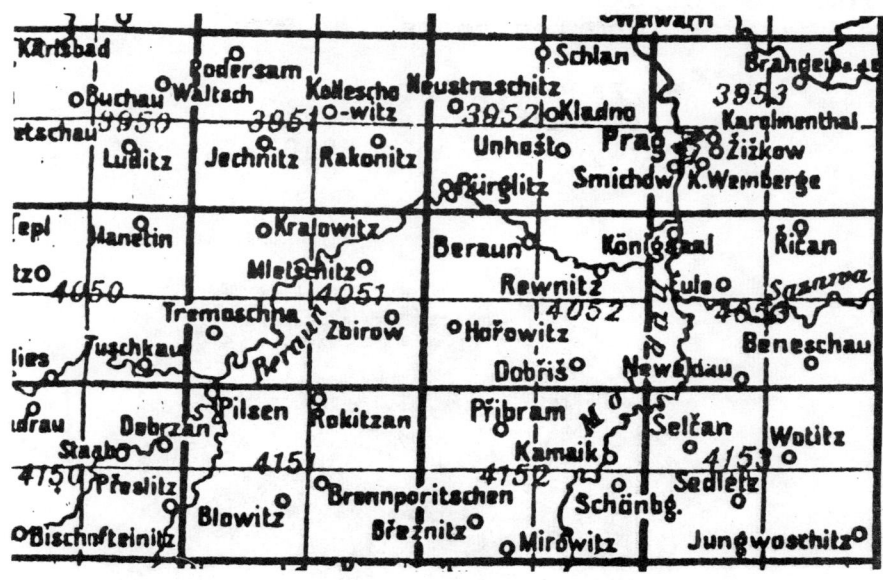

NO. 20. ENLARGED SECTION OF MAP GRID OVERVIEW.

Example: Prague is on map number 3953.

Convenient maps of several individual old Hungarian counties are available on film no. 1,181,575, item 2. These include the following counties, all or part of which are now in Czechoslovakia: Abauj-Torna, Pozsony, Gömör, Hont, Komarom, Nyitra, Nograd, Esztergom, Gyor, and Zemplen (see illustration no. 21). If available for the county (megye) in which you are researching, these maps can be of considerable help since they are quite detailed and legible. District boundaries on these maps are not the same as given in the Hungarian gazetteer of 1877. Also, as explained before, many place names will differ from the gazetteer.

Excellent pre-World War II sectional maps (1:200,000) are available for Czechoslovakia and other middle European countries from the following company:

>Genealogy Unlimited, Inc.
>789 South Buffalo Grove Road
>Buffalo Grove, Illinois 60089

<u>Auto Atlas CSSR</u> [Auto Atlas of the Czechoslovak Socialist Republic], Bratislava: Slovenska kartografia, 1971, reprinted every few years (Ref. 943.7 E3a, not filmed), contains modern 1:400,000 maps of Czechoslovakia. All place names are in Czech

and Slovak. There is an index on pages 147-169. It is available at the Genealogical Library but is under copyright and cannot be microfilmed. This atlas is reprinted periodically and might be available from the following company or from any other store that deals in Czechoslovak imported books.

F. Pancner, Inc.
6514 West Cermak Road
Berwyn, Illinois 60402

Bohemian cottage.

Bohemian manor farm.

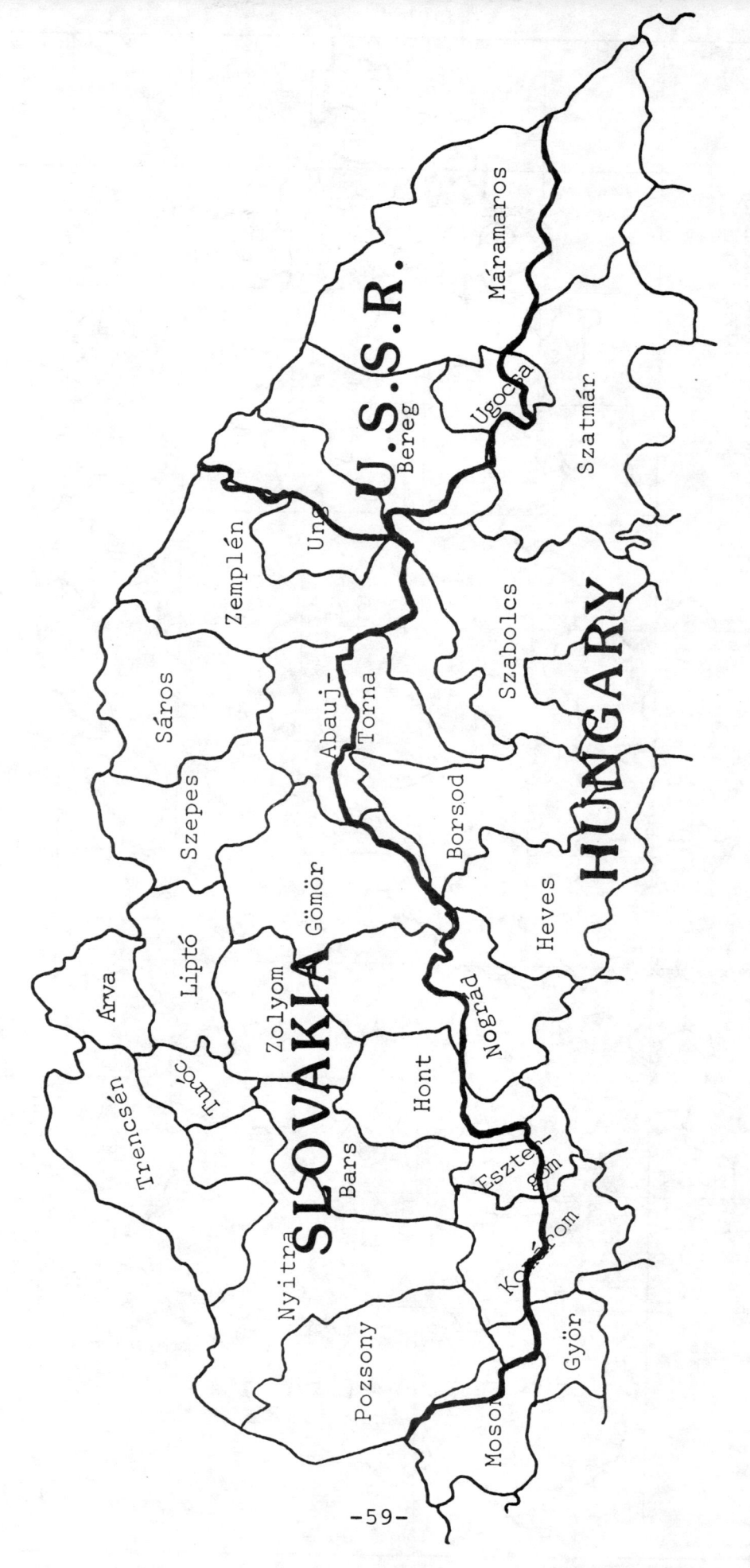

NO. 21. OLD HUNGARIAN COUNTIES (MEGYE) NOW IN CZECHOSLOVAKIA AND THE SOVIET UNION.

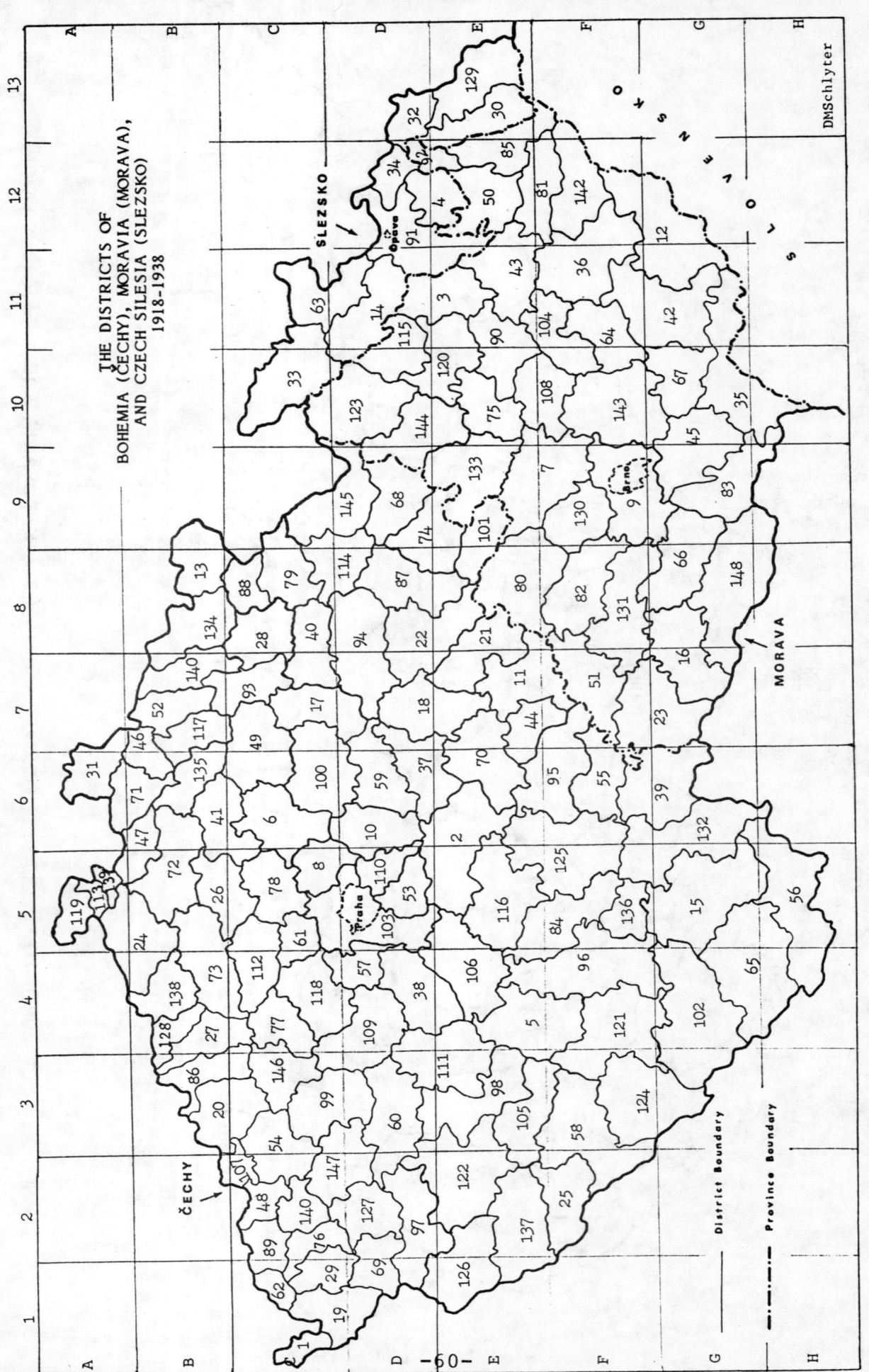

NO. 22. THE DISTRICTS OF BOHEMIA (ČECHY), MORAVIA (MORAVA), AND CZECH SILESIA (SLEZSKO), 1918-1938.

THE DISTRICTS OF BOHEMIA, MORAVIA, AND SILESIA
1918 - 1939
(C) = Čechy   (M) = Morava   (S) = Slezsko

1. Aš, Asch, (C) C-1
   Auspitz, see 45
   Aussig, see 138
   Bärn, see 3
2. Benešov, Beneschau (C) E-6
3. Moravský Beroun, Bärn (M) E-11
4. Bílovec, Wagstadt (S) E-12
   Bischofteinitz, see 137
5. Blatná (C) E-4
6. Mladá Boleslav, Jung-Bunzlau (C) C-6
   Böhmisch Brod, see 10
   Böhmisch Budweis, see 15
   Böhmisch Krumau, see 65
   Böhmisch Leipa, see 72
7. Boskovice, Boskowitz (M) F-9
8. Brandýs nad Labem, Brandeis (C) C-5
   Braunau, see 13
9. Brno, Brünn (M) F-9
10. Český Brod, Böhmisch Brod (C) D-6
11. Německý Brod, Deutsch Brod, now Havlíčkův Brod (C) E-7
12. Uherský Brod, Ungarisch Brod (M) G-12
13. Broumov, Braunau (C) B-8
    Brünn, see 9
14. Bruntál, Freudenthal (S) D-11
    Brüx, see 86
15. České Budějovice, Böhmisch Budweis (C) G-5
16. Moravské Budějovice, Mährisch Budweis (M) G-7
17. Nový Bydžov, Neu-Bydžov (C) C-7
18. Čáslav, Tschaslau (C) D-7
    Česká Lipa, see 72
    České Budějovice, see 15
    Český Brod, see 10
    Český Krumlov, see 65
    Český Těšín, see 129
19. Cheb, Eger (C) C-1

20. Chomutov, Komotau (C) B-3
21. Chotěboř (C) E-8
22. Chrudim (C) D-8
23. Dačice, Datschitz (M) G-7
    Dauba, see 26
24. Děčín, Tetschen (C) B-5
    Deutsch Brod, see 11
    Deutsch Gabel, see 47
25. Domažlice, Taus (C) F-2
26. Dubá, Dauba (C) B-5
27. Duchcov, Dux (C) B-4
28. Dvůr Králové nad Labem, Königinhof a.d. Elbe (C) C-8
    Eger, see 19
    Elbogen, see 76
    Eule, see 53
29. Falknov nad Ohří, Falkenau a.d. Eger (C) C-1
    Freistadt, see 32
    Freiwaldau, see 33
    Freudenthal, see 14
    Friedeck, see 30
    Friedland, see 31
30. Frýdek, Friedeck (S) E-13
31. Frýdlant, Friedland (C) A-6
32. Fryštát, Freistadt, now Karviná, Karwin (S) D-13
33. Frývaldov, Freiwaldau, now Jeseník (S) C-10
    Gablonz a.d. Neisse, see 46
    Gaya, see 67
    Göding, see 35
    Graslitz, see 62
    Gross Meseritsch, see 82
    Havlíčkův Brod, see 11
34. Hlučín, Hultschin (S) D-12
35. Hodonín, Göding (M) G-10
    Hohenelbe, see 141
    Hohenmauth, see 87
    Hohenstadt, see 144
36. Holešov, Holleschau (M) F-11
37. Kutná Hora, Kuttenberg (C) D-6

-61-

38. Hořovice (C) D-4
39. Jindřichův Hradec, Neuhaus (C) G-6
    Horšovský Týn, see 137
40. Hradec Králové, Königgrätz (C) C-8
41. Mnichovo Hradiště, Münchengrätz (C) B-6
42. Uherské Hradiště, Ungarisch Hradisch (M) G-11
43. Hranice, Mährisch Weisskirchen (M) E-11
    Hultschin, see 34
44. Humpolec (C) E-7
45. Hustopeče, Auspitz (M) G-10
    Iglau, see 51
46. Jablonec nad Nisou, Gablonz a.d. Neisse (C) B-7
47. Německé Jablonné, Deutsch Gabel, now Jablonne v Podještědi (C) B-6
48. Jáchymov, Sankt Joachimsthal (C) C-2
    Jägerndorf, see 63
    Jeseník, see 33
49. Jičín, Jitschin (C) C-7
50. Nový Jičín, Neu-Titschein (M) E-12
51. Jihlava, Iglau (M) F-7
52. Jílemnice, Starkenbach (C) B-7
53. Jílové, Eule (C) D-5
    Jindřichův Hradec, see 39
    Jitschin, see 49
    Joachimsthal, see 48
    Jung-Bunzlau, see 6
54. Kadaň, Kaadan (C) C-3
55. Kamenice nad Lipou, Kamenitz (C) F-6
56. Kaplice, Kaplitz (C) H-5
    Karlovy Vary, see 140
    Karlsbad, see 140
    Karviná, Karwin, see 32
57. Kladno (C) D-4
58. Klatovy, Klattau (C) F-3
59. Kolín (C) D-6
    Komotau, see 20
    Königgrätz, see 40
    Königinhof a.d. Elbe, see 28
    Králové Dvůr, see 28
60. Kralovice, Kralowitz (C) D-3
61. Kralupy nad Vltavou, Kralup (C) C-5
62. Kraslice, Graslitz (C) C-1
    Kremsier, see 64
63. Krnov, Jägerndorf (S) C-11
64. Kroměříž, Kremsier (M) F-11
65. Český Krumlov, Böhmisch Krumau (C) G-4
66. Moravský Krumlov, Mährisch Kromau (M) G-8
    Kutná Hora, see 37
    Kuttenberg, see 37
67. Kyjov, Gaya (M) G-10
68. Lanškroun, Landskron (C) D-9
    Laun, see 77
69. Mariánské Lázně, Marienbad (C) D-1
70. Ledeč nad Sázavou, Ledetsch (C) E-6
    Leitmeritz, see 73
    Leitomischl, see 74
71. Liberec, Reichenberg (C) B-6
72. Česká Lípa, Böhmisch Leipa (C) B-5
73. Litoměřice, Leitmeritz (C) B-4
74. Litomyšl, Leitomischl (C) D-9
75. Litovel, Littau (M) E-10
76. Loket, Elbogen (C) C-2
77. Louny, Laun (C) C-4
    Luditz, see 147
    Mährisch Budweis, see 16
    Mährisch Kromau, see 66
    Mährisch Ostrau, see 92
    Mährisch Schönberg, see 123
    Mährisch Trübau, see 133
    Mährisch Weisskirchen, see 43
    Mariánské Lázně, see 69
    Marienbad, see 69
78. Mělník (C) C-5
79. Nové Město nad Metují, Neustadt a.d. Mettau (C) C-8
80. Nové Město na Moravě, Neustadt, Neustadtl (M) E-8
81. Valašske Meziříčí, Wallachisch Meseritsch (M) F-12

82. Velké Meziříčí, Gross Meseritsch (M) F-8
Mies, see 122
83. Mikulov, Nikolsburg (M) G-9
84. Milevsko, Mühlhausen (C) F-5
85. Místek (M) E-12
Mladá Boleslav, see 6
Mnichovo Hradiště, see 41
Moldauthein, see 136
Moravská Ostrava, see 92
Moravská Třebová, see 133
Moravské Budějovice, see 16
Moravský Beroun, see 3
Moravský Krumlov, see 66
86. Most, Brüx (C) B-3
Mühlhausen, see 84
Münchengrätz, see 41
87. Vysoké Mýto, Hohenmauth (C) D-8
88. Náchod (C) C-8
89. Nejdek, Neudeck (C) C-2
Německé Jablonné, see 47
Německý Brod, see 11
Neu-Bydzov, see 17
Neudeck, see 89
Neuhaus, see 39
Neupaka, see 93
Neustadt a.d. Mettau, see 79
Neustadt, Neustadtl, see 80
Neu-Titschein, see 50
Nikolsburg, see 83
Nová Paka, see 93
Nové Město nad Metují, see 79
Nové Město na Moravě, see 80
Nový Bydžov, see 17
Nový Jičín, see 50
90. Olomouc, Olmutz (M) E-11
91. Opava, Troppau (S) D-12
92. Moravská Ostrava, Mährisch Ostrau (M) D-12
93. Nová Paka, Neupaka (C) C-7
94. Pardubice, Pardubitz (C) D-8
95. Pelhřimov, Pilgram (C) F-6
Pilsen, see 98
96. Písek (C) F-4
97. Planá, Plan (C) D-2
98. Plzeň, Pilsen (C) E-3
99. Podbořany, Podersam (C) C-3
100. Poděbrady, Podiebrad (C) C-6
Podersam, see 99
Podiebrad, see 100
101. Polička (C) E-9
102. Prachatice, Prachatitz (C) G-4
103. Praha, Prag, Prague (C) D-5
104. Přerov, Prerau (M) F-11
Pressnitz, see 107
105. Prestice (C) E-3
106. Příbram (C) E-4
107. Přísečnice, Pressnitz (C) C-2
108. Prostějov, Prossnitz (M) F-10
109. Rakovník, Rakonitz (C) D-4
Raudnitz a.d. Elbe, see 112
Reichenau a.d. Kněžna, see 114
Reichenberg, see 71
110. Říčany (C) D-5
111. Rokycany, Rokytzan (C) D-3
Römerstadt, see 115
112. Roudnice nad Labem, Raudnitz a.d. Elbe (C) C-4
113. Rumburk, Rumberg (C) A-5
114. Rychnov, Reichenau a.d. Knezna (C) D-8
115. Rymarov, Römerstadt (M) D-11
Saaz, see 146
Sankt Joachimsthal, see 48
Schlan, see 118
Schluckenau, see 119
Schüttenhofen, see 124
116. Sedlčany (C) E-5
117. Semily, Semil (C) B-7
Senftenberg, see 145
118. Slaný, Schlan (C) C-4
119. Šluknov, Schluckenau (C) A-5
Starkenbach, see 52
120. Šternberk, Sternberg (M) E-10
121. Strakonice, Strakonitz (C) F-4
122. Stříbro, Mies (C) E-2
123. Šumperk, Mährisch Schönberg (M) D-10
124. Sušice, Schüttenhofen

(C) F-3
125. Tábor (C) F-5
126. Tchov, Tachau (C) E-1
Taus, see 25
127. Teplá, Tepl (C) D-2
128. Teplice-Šanov, Teplitz-Schönau, now Teplice, Teplitz (C) B-4
129. Český Těšín, Tschechisch Teschen (S) E-13
Tetschen, see 24
130. Tišnov, Tischnowitz (M) F-9
Trautenau, see 134
131. Třebíč, Trebitsch (M) F-8
132. Třeboň, Wittingau (C) G-6
133. Moravská Třebová, Mährisch Trübau (M) E-9
Troppau, see 91
134. Trutnov, Trautenau (C) B-8
Tschaslau, see 18
Tschechisch Teschen, see 129
135. Turnov, Turnau (C) B-6
136. Týn nad Vltavou, Moldauthein (C) F-5
137. Horšovský Týn, Bischofteinitz (C) E-2
Uherské Hradiště, see 42
Uherský Brod, see 12
Ungarisch Brod, see 12
Ungarisch Hradisch, see 42
138. Ústí nad Labem, Aussig (C) B-4
Valašské Meziříčí, see 81
139. Varnsdorf, Warnsdorf (C) A-5
140. Karlovy Vary, Karlsbad (C) C-2
Velké Meziříčí, see 82
141. Vrchlabí, Hohenelbe (C) B-7
142. Vsetín, Wsetin (M) F-12
143. Vyškov, Wischau (M) F-10
Vysoké Mýto, see 87
Wagstadt, see 4
Wallachisch Meseritsch, see 81
Warnsdorf, see 139
Wischau, see 143
Wittingau, see 132
Wsetin, see 142
144. Zábřeh, Hohenstadt (M) D-10
145. Žamberk, Senftenberg (C) D-9
146. Žatec, Saaz (C) D-3
147. Žlutice, Luditz (C) C-2
148. Znojmo, Znaim (M) G-8

Bohemian national costumes.

CHAPTER 6

GENEALOGICAL RESEARCH BY CORRESPONDENCE

Genealogical research is not possible without using primary genealogical sources, especially vital records of births, marriages, and deaths. Aside from a few census returns from limited areas of Slovakia, which were filmed in Hungary, no Czechoslovak genealogical sources are available in this country. The LDS Genealogical Library in Salt Lake City, which has gathered the greatest assemblage of genealogical source material in the world, has not yet been able to microfilm records in Czechoslovak archives. When records of Czechoslovakia eventually are microfilmed, the author plans a supplement or revised edition of this book to explain research procedures.

Fortunately, genealogical research can be done by correspondence, in the English language, with the Czechoslovak Embassy in Washington, D.C., or, for non-Americans, with the Archival Agency in Prague. Czechoslovakia is one of the few countries in the world that has made provisions for genealogical research by foreigners. The Embassy transmits requests for research to appropriate archives in Czechoslovakia, where qualified archival researchers undertake the actual research. Reports are then returned to the applicants through the Embassy. Persons in the United States who want genealogical searches of old Czechoslovak records should apply to the Czechoslovak Embassy:

    Embassy of the Czechoslovak Socialist Republic
    Consular Division
    3900 Linnean Avenue, N.W.
    Washington, D.C. 20008

Canadian residents should request an application from the Czechoslovak Consulate in Montreal:

    Consulate of the Czechoslovak Socialist Republic
    1305 Pine Avenue
    Montreal, Quebec H3G 1B2

Persons living outside the United States and Canada should apply directly to the Archival Administration in Prague:

    Archivní Správa
    160 00 Praha 6
    Tř. Obranců míru 133
    Czechoslovakia

Genealogists are fortunate that provisions have been made for research through this office since it is not advisable to ask friends or relatives in Czechoslovakia to do the research. Czechoslovak archives are open to the public, but the law specifies that visitors may work only on their own ancestry. It is strictly forbidden for Czechoslovak citizens to send material copied from the archives out of the country; violation of this law could cause the offender serious trouble. Also, it takes a skilled researcher to read the old records which are handwritten in several languages, a skill usually beyond the ability of all but experienced researchers. Do not try to hire private archival personnel; such action will cause trouble for the archivist and can lead to real problems for the genealogist, both in poor-quality research and in future relations with the archive. By working through proper channels, you have the protection of being able to dispute possible errors and, if necessary, request that the work be redone. Thus, correspondence with individual archives is strongly discouraged. Most employees of individual archives do not have sufficient time or competency with the English language to answer inquiries.

All parish registers and other genealogical sources in Czechoslovakia have been consolidated. The more current records are at local and parish offices; older ones are kept in more centralized regional archives. Although inventories of most archival vital records holdings are available (see Appendix B), it is not always possible to determine where specific records will be found, especially the more recent ones. By working through the Embassy and the Archival Administration, you can be sure that requests reach the proper archive.

Research can be undertaken only when you provide basic information. You must provide the name and at least an approximate birth date of your immigrant ancestor. If the ancestor was married in the old country, it may be possible to start with the marriage date. It is essential that you give the specific place where the birth or marriage occurred because these records were kept at the local level.

The Czechoslovak Archival Administration provides two types of research:

1. <u>Individual birth, marriage, and death certificates</u>. These records include certificates of births, marriages, and deaths, written in Czech or Slovak, on forms presently being used in Czechoslovakia. These documents can be easier to read than those provided by the "running-account" research described below, but they often contain less information. The certificate fee, usually $10.00 per document, sometimes will be higher because of difficulties in research due to lack of details or inaccuracy in the information you provide.

2. <u>Genealogical research in the form of a running account</u>. This method of research reports information exactly as found

in the original record (German, Latin, Hungarian, Czech, or Slovak). Sometimes all information is listed only in Czech or Slovak. Comments by the researcher are given in Czech or Slovak. The fee for research is based on the time spent: $12.00 per hour (subject to change). Photocopies of actual documents cannot be provided.

A major advantage of the "running account" is that the report details exactly which records were searched. Valuable and interesting bits of information may be included that normally would be omitted from certificates. These details provide better and more thorough research and make your genealogy more than just a list of names. The "running-account" format is less expensive because it eliminates the cost of unnecessary certification. The disadvantage of this format is that reports are often long and involved. Because of the complexities of Czech and Slovak grammar, names of people and places may be altered slightly, which can be confusing to persons not familiar with the languages.

While the certificates also are in Czech or Slovak, they are less grammatically complex than a running-account report. However, the certificates do not provide details about the family, other marriages, or movement from another town, etc. Also, they do not provide an accounting of the research process. These disadvantages far outweigh the small advantage of grammatical simplicity.

The actual research is done by archival employees. The work is apt to be time consuming, especially when exact dates are not known. A great deal of information sometimes can be found in only a few hours; in other cases, results of extensive and expensive research are very limited. Some lines can be traced in detail back to the seventeenth century. In other cases, little can be done because clues leading to earlier ancestors do not appear in the records. It is not possible to estimate costs in advance. Keep in mind that the fee is for time spent in doing research and not for results obtained.

A request to "trace the family line back as far as possible" could result in hundreds of records in a few generations and could cost hundreds of dollars. It is advisable to set a limit on costs when making your first application. The Embassy requests an advance deposit of $50.00 (more if a large number of records are to be searched) by cashier's check or money order payable to the Czechoslovak Embassy. The fee will be adjusted when the results of the research are known. If you are not certain as to the accuracy of the locality, or if you have doubts as to the existence of records, you may want to request one birth certificate at $10.00. If nothing is found, it has cost you only $10.00; but if other records are discovered, you can proceed with a full-scale research effort using the "running-account" method. This approach is slow, taking six months or longer for the first reply and another six months for the actual research.

Velvyslanectví Československé Socialistické Republiky
Embassy of the Czechoslovak Socialist Republic
3900 Linnean Avenue, N.W.
Washington, D.C. 20008

APPLICATION FOR INDIVIDUAL CERTIFICATE OF BIRTH, MARRIAGE, OR DEATH

ŽÁDOST O JEDNOTLIVÝ VÝPIS Z MATRIK NAROZENÍ, SŇATKŮ, nebo ÚMRTÍ

==

Reference/file number of any previous correspondence with Czechoslovak Embassy: _____

1. Name and address of applicant: _____
   _____
   _____

2. Type of certificate requested: ☐ Birth   ☐ Marriage   ☐ Death
                                   Rodný List   Oddací List   Úmrtní List

3. Name of person to be researched: _____

   Date of birth/marriage/death: _____

   Place/Village/Town: _____ County: _____

   Name of Father: _____

   Maiden name of mother: _____

   Name of spouse: _____

   Religion: _____

4. Additional information about person to be researched: _____
   _____
   _____
   _____

5. Sources:

Deposit: $_____   Limit (if any): $_____   Date: _____

Additional comments:

APPLICATION FOR GENEALOGICAL RESEARCH
IN THE FORM OF RUNNING ACCOUNT

ŽÁDOST O VYHLEDÁNÍ NAVAZUJÍCÍCH
GENEALOGICKÝCH INFORMACÍ OBSAHUJÍCÍCH PLNÉ VÝPISY Z MATRIK

===

Reference/file number of any previous correspondence with Czechoslovakia Embassy: _____

1. Name and address of applicant: _____
   _____
   _____

2. Name of person to be researched: _____

   Date of birth: _____

   Place of birth (specific town or village): _____

   Further identify the birthplace with the name of the county, the parish or a larger town nearby: _____

   Name of father: _____

   Maiden name of mother: _____

   Religion: _____

   • The most important items are name, date, and place. The date can be a close approximation.

3. Other information available about the person (such as date and place of death, if the death occurred in Czechoslovakia): _____
   _____

4. Relatives of the person being researched. (This is optional but often very helpful.)
   a) Husband or Wife
      Name: Date of birth: Place:
                               Date of marriage: Place:

   b) Children
      Name: Date of birth: Place:

   c) Brothers and Sisters
      Name: Date of birth: Place:

5. Sources:

☐ Please provide birth dates of all brothers and sisters of direct-line ancestors.
  Prosím, vyhledejte též narození všech sourozenců přímých předků.

☐ Please research direct-line ancestors only.
  Prosím, vyhledejte pouze předky přímých linek.

Deposit: $_____   Limit (if any): $_____   Date: _____

Additional Comments:

The Embassy in Washington, D.C., prefers that the request for research be made on an application form. A letter detailing a genealogical request can become very involved and complex. The application form makes it possible to state your request in a manner easily understood. Separate applications for each type of research are shown on pages 68 and 69. Xerox and use the appropriate form for the type of research wanted: certificates or "running account."

The application should be kept simple. You should request only one ancestral line at a time. Be sure to indicate whether you want information about brothers and sisters of your direct ancestors or whether you prefer to receive information only regarding your direct line. The form provided has a box that can be checked to indicate your wishes. Providing as much accurate information as possible will increase the chances for success, but do not assume that you are expected to fill in every space. If exact dates are not known, you should estimate. Indicating religion is very helpful, especially if the ancestor was non-Catholic.

It is essential that you give the place of birth or marriage. You must thoroughly identify the locality. If you have found the locality in one of the gazetteers described in Chapter 5, indicate the name of the political district or enclose a photocopy of the gazetteer entry. Also, if you know the location of the parish or synagogue, include this as well. If you cannot check the gazetteers yourself, you can try letting the archive researchers find your locality; but remember, they may not have access to all the gazetteers described in this book, and they must charge for their research time. To help them, provide all information you have about the geographical location, such as the name of a nearby larger town, or send a photocopy of an old Austrian or Hungarian document if you have nothing else. These items of information will give clues that may help identify the correct locale, a step of great importance since there often are many localities with the same place name. Problems involving misspelled or non-Czechoslovak place names often can be solved when sufficient extra information is provided. If the problem is too complex, it may be necessary to get expert help by hiring an accredited genealogist.

If the nature of your request does not fit the format of the application form, you will need to compose a letter. Keep your letter as simple as possible; come directly to the point. Remember, those who read your letter may have little experience with the complexities of the English language. Be sure all localities are clearly indicated and that dates and relationships are not confusing. You may want to simplify your request using a form of your own making.

Be sure to keep a copy of your completed application for future reference. This precaution will enable you to remember exactly what was requested and when. When you get your reply, check to see whether your instructions were properly followed. Examples of certificates and of a report in the form of a "running account" are provided on the following pages. Such archival reports are in Czechoslovakia and are, therefore, in Czech or Slovak. The Embassy does not provide a translation service. Chapter 8 deals with these languages and may help in translation. In addition, you may need the help of someone qualified in the language. A list of accredited, professional genealogical researchers may be obtained from the LDS Genealogical Library.

When you receive your report from the Embassy, organize the information by placing it on a pedigee (family tree) chart. Using this chart as a guide, you can clearly visualize what research has been done and then decide how you want to proceed. Do you want to go further on the mother's side of the family or continue on the father's side? Do you need the marriage date of the mother's parents? Is there a second marriage about which you want more information? Do you want further data on brothers and sisters? Carefully evaluate what additional research is to be done and then write again. In this manner you can proceed with two or three generations at a time. Each correspondence may add a new limb to your family tree, spreading the cost of research over many months or years depending on the pace you set.

Sometimes it is essential to be persistent. If an archive indicates the necessary records are not available, you may want to try again in six months or a year. Often the archival researchers will find records the second time which, for various reasons, they were unable to find the first time. This apparent inconsistency raises an obvious question: How well do the archival researchers do their job? Experience has shown that the quality of research can vary greatly. Basically the quality depends on the archivist. For some, genealogical research is unenjoyable and a distraction from other archival projects. Other archivists are diligent researchers and are willing to spend the time and effort necessary to do a better job.

Several problems may arise in the course of your dealings with the Embassy and archival researchers:

1. Your specific instructions may not be followed. Despite your request that the research include names and birth dates of brothers and sisters of your ancestors, the archivist may research only the direct line. When filling out your request form, if you want brothers and sisters, it is a good idea not only to check the box requesting such information but also to circle it in bright red ink. Whenever specific instructions are given, such as "follow only the paternal line," be sure that they are clearly expressed.

2. The format of the various reports is not consistent. Each archivist may report the information he finds as he wishes. The official definition of a "running account" states that

the information will be reported as found in the original records. Commentary is at the discretion of the researcher. Occasionally reports are received which are mere name lists or family trees without dates, places, or sources. If you receive such a report, you should send a copy of the original request and the report to the Embassy with a demand that the research be redone.

3. Often simple research procedures are not followed. For example, as a line is traced, the archivist may be unable to find the birth record of a specific ancestor in the records of the parish checked. The proper procedure in such cases is to check the records of all neighboring parishes for the birth. Since people moved very little in earlier centuries, this technique usually will locate the ancestor. But the procedure requires extra thought and effort, and many archival researchers will not undertake it. As another example, when two or more persons are found with the same name, born in the same time period, it can be difficult to determine which is the direct ancestor. A careful researcher can solve the problem by comparing brothers and sisters with the names of witnesses who appear at later christenings in the family. This requires a lot of thought and time and is almost never done. The archival researchers often are quick to give up on a difficult line and pick an easier one. Many times the most effective way of researching is to find all entries pertaining to a given surname and then fit them together later. It is difficult to get them to do this for you.

4. It is possible that the researchers will exaggerate the complexity of the research, taking more time than is realistically necessary to find the needed information, which results in greater expense. This is especially true in times of economic difficulties in Czechoslovakia when western currencies are desperately needed to strengthen the economy. Because some genealogical procedures are time-consuming enough without exaggeration, you will find that the cost of specifically requesting certain careful genealogical research procedures will place them out of practical reach.

Since these problems exist, you may wish to consider the following alternatives:

1. It is possible for you personally to do research in the Czechoslovak archives. This should not be considered, however, unless you have experience in working with old handwritten records and know Czech or German. A knowledge of Latin also is almost essential. When writing for your visa you should specify that you are interested in visiting the archives to do genealogical research. You should have permission to use the archives before you leave the United States. This groundwork can take a lot of time, so you should start early. If you are short on time, it may be

possible to obtain permission in Prague at the State Archival Administration offices located at Obrancǔ mĭru 133, Praha 6, near the Hradčanská metro station. Leave the station through the exit marked Prazský Hrad, turn left, and then walk two blocks to the Archivní Sprava building.

Be forewarned that using the archives personally can be a frustrating and time-consuming experience. Some archives have very helpful personnel who will assist you as much as possible; other archives may give you no help at all. No photocopying facilities are available and photographs are forbidden. The hours the archives are open are often irregular. An archive may simply shut down for weeks or months at a time for such reasons as taking inventory, making repairs, or lack of fuel for heating.

2. If you are unable to go to the archives yourself, you may consider sending a qualified and trustworthy researcher into Czechoslovakia. This can be quite expensive. Nevertheless, it may prove to be well worth the expense and, in the long run, be less expensive than using the official channels. One must exercise the utmost caution in considering such a step. There are many unscrupulous individuals in Austria and Germany who offer their services for this kind of research. Fabricated genealogies and poor-quality research are common. The best course to follow, if you cannot do the research personally, is to send someone you know and trust, or rely on the services of the Embassy.

3. Eventually, it is hoped, the records of Czechoslovakia will be microfilmed and made available through the Genealogical Library and its branches. Until genealogical source material is made available on microfilm in this country, the Embassy and archival staff researchers remain the most viable means of research, despite their shortcomings.

Seal of the Czechoslovak Republic.

NO. 25. INDIVIDUALLY ISSUED CERTIFICATES ON FORMS NOW IN USE IN CZECHOSLOVAKIA.

Birth Certificate (in Czech)

Marriage Certificate (in Slovak)

Death Certificate (in Czech)

The following example shows an extract from the birth register of Říčany for Anežka Kumstová which was copied directly from the original record with commentary by the researcher. The format of archival reports will vary depending on the style of the researcher making the report.

STÁTNÍ OBLASTNÍ ARCHIV V PRAZE
128 00 Praha 2, Horská 7

Čj. Sar - 1198/60-1979
Při odpovědi uveďte vždy toto číslo jednací!

V Praze dne 25.11.1980

Mr. Adolph Novak

U.S.A.

Vážený pane,

zasíláme Vám zbývající část genealogických údajů o Vašich předcích. Některé se nám nepodařilo zjistit, zvláště proto, že mladší matriky nejsou dosud uloženy v našem archivu. Rovněž nelze zjistit nic o původu Augustina Šmída, děda Anežky Kumstové, poněvadž byl nalezencem z Pražské porodnice č.1107 a byl pouze vychován Tomášem Vojáčkem, obuvníkem z Tehova. Jeho skuteční rodiče jsou pochopitelně neznámí.

Anežka Kumstová se narodila 19.11.1888. Její narození je podle sdělení matričního obvodu v Říčanech zapsáno v matrice narozených římsko katolického farního úřadu (dále již jen ř.k.f.ú.) Říčany ve svazku X. na straně 127:

Den, měsíc a rok narození:	19.11.1888
Místo narození:	Tehov čp.33
Jméno a příjmení dítěte:	Anežka Kumstová
Pohlaví:	ženské
Náboženství:	katolické
Otec:	Josef Kumsta, dělník v Tehově čp.33, syn Václava Kumsty, chalupníka v Tehově čp.5 a Marie rozené Trojánkové z Tehova
Matka:	Anna, dcera Augustina Šmída, obuvníka v Tehově čp.33 a matky Barbory rozené Lulové z Tehova

A. Rodina Kumstova. Jméno se v zápisech objevuje ve dvojí formě, a to jak Kumst, tak Kumsta. Častější je forma Kumsta, takže jsme se k ní rovněž přiklonili.

1. Otec Anežky Kumstové, provdané Dražilové, byl Josef Kumsta. Narodil se v Tehově 17.12.1862, jak vyplývá z údajů uváděných při

NO. 26. FIRST PAGE OF A NINE-PAGE ARCHIVAL REPORT.

The example shown here is taken from an archival report. It gives the birth and marriage record for Václav Dražil in Latin and his death record in Czech. Note the use of Latin Wenceslaus for Václav and the use of the spelling Drazyl for Dražil in the original marriage record.

Václav Dražil, otec Jakuba Dražila, se narodil podle zápisu v matrice tripartitní ř.k.f.ú. Říčany, sign M 22-1/2 na fol. 66 dne 9.7.1742:

9. Julii 1742 natus, 10.baptizatus. Ego Wenceslaus Ferdinandus Kořil, loci curatus, baptizavi .... Wenceslaum, patris Joannis Dražil ex pago Tehov, matris Annae, subditi Kostelaczium, ...

Oženil se dne 26.1.1766 z Kateřinou Rezkovou z Tehova. Zápis o sňatku se nachází v matrice tripartitní ř.k.f.ú. Říčany, sign. M 22-1/5 na pag. 53:

A[nno] D[omi]ni 1766 die 26. Mense Januario contraxit matrimonium per verba de presenti honestus sponsus Wenceslaus, filius Joannis Drazyl, gazarii ex pago Tehov cum honesta sponsa Catharina, filia post defunctum Paulum Rezek, gazarium ex eodem pago, ...

Zemřel dne 25.1.1807 v Tehově. Zápis o úmrtí byl učiněn do matriky zemřelých ř.k.f.ú. Říčany, sign. M 22-1/15 na pag. 15:

Měsíc, rok a den:	Januarius, roku 1807, 25.zemřel, 27.pohřben
Nro. domu:	[Tehov] čp.7
Jméno zemřelého:	Václav Dražil, výminkář z Tehova
Náboženství:	katolického
Pohlaví:	mužského
Věku:	70 [!]
Způsob nemoci a smrti:	slabostí těla a stářím

NO. 27. A BIRTH AND MARRIAGE RECORD FROM AN ARCHIVAL REPORT.

TRANSLATION OF BIRTH AND MARRIAGE RECORD (NO. 27)

Václav Dražil, father of Jakub Dražil, was born according to the entry in the parish register of Říčany Roman Catholic parish (M22-1/2) on page 66, on 9 July 1742:

9 July 1742 born, 10th baptized. I Wenceslaus Fernandus Kořil, curate of this place, baptized .... Wenceslaus, of the father Joannes Dražil from the village of Tehov, of the mother Anna, serfs of Kostelec, ...

He married on 26 Jan 1766 with Kateřina Rezková of Tehov. The entry of the marriage was found in the parish register of Roman Catholic parish of Říčany (M22-1/5) on page 53.

Year of our Lord 1766 the 26th day of the month of January was contracted matrimony of the honest groom Wenceslaus, son of Joannes Drazyl, tanner from village of Tehov with the honest bride Catharina, daughter of the deceased Paulus Rezek, tanner of the same village, ...

He died on 25 Jan 1807 in Tehov. The entry of the death was put into the register of the Roman Catholic parish of Říčany (M22-1/15) on page 15:

Month, year and day:	January 1807, 25th died, 27th buried
House number:	[Tehov] #7
Name of deceased:	Václav Dražil, pensioner of Tehov
Religion:	Catholic
Sex:	Male
Age:	70 [sic!]
Cause of sickness and death:	Weakness of body and age

The next section of this archival report (not illustrated) explains that a search of the parish of Říčany failed to produce a birth date for the wife, Kateřina, but that she was found in the nearby parish of Sluštice. She and her family moved into Tehov in the year 1751. This is an example of a careful search of nearby parishes done by a conscientious archival researcher.

CHAPTER 7

SOURCES IN CZECHOSLOVAKIA

Genealogical research is not a simple matter of looking up your family in a book or on a computer. It is a painstaking process of consulting original records to determine dates, places, events, and other information about ancestors in order to construct an accurate record. You must proceed carefully from one generation to the next.

VITAL RECORDS

The primary sources for genealogical research in Czechoslovakia are records of christening, marriage, and death kept by local clergy. These parish registers [matriky] are called vital records.

The first official decree requiring Catholic clergy to keep records of christenings in their parishes was issued by the Council of Trent in 1563. Some areas in what is now Czechoslovakia began keeping records even earlier than this. Fragments of a few such records are all that now exist for that early era. Most parishes did not keep records until the 1600s despite encouragement and directives to do so. In 1614 the church issued the so-called Ritual Romanorum. This act provided examples to assist the clergy in understanding what was expected, including the recording of christenings, marriages, and burials. Thus, the practice of record keeping was accepted gradually so that by 1700 four out of five Catholic parishes were following this directive.

Some Protestant clergy began keeping records as early as the fifteenth century, but these have been lost. Harsh Catholization measures, initiated in the Czech lands after the battle of White Mountain in 1620, caused the loss of most Protestant records. The records of Čeliv parish, near Plzeň, date from 1614. Remarks written in the register by the Protestant pastor who kept the record from 1614 to 1624 indicate that he was forced to abandon the parish for a period of time in 1620, during which time the earlier records were lost. In 1630 the new Catholic priest remarked that his predecessor was a "seducer of the peasants, a most wicked Lutheran, may his soul roast in hell."

After 1624 Protestantism was prohibited in the Czech lands, and Protestants were severely persecuted. The Protestant clergy were officially expelled, and their parishes were taken over by Catholic priests. Protestants were not legally permitted to perform christenings or marriages, but had to go to the Catholic priests. Thus, Protestant christenings, marriages, and deaths will be in the Catholic registers. Some Protestant individuals, however, refused Catholic authority and were not recorded.

Catholicism was the only religion permitted in Austria until 1 May 1781 when Emperor Josef II issued the Edict of Toleration. This edict extended to Protestants and Jews the right to meet openly and keep their own records. After more than 150 years of persecution, Protestant congregations were comparatively few; nevertheless, most began keeping their own records shortly after the edict was issued. It was not until 1849, however, that Protestants were permitted to maintain their own registers without Catholic supervision.

The Counter-Reformation efforts of the Habsburgs were not so successful in Slovakia, which was under Hungarian administration. Hungary, at the Peace of Linz in 1645, succeeded in forcing the Habsburgs to reaffirm certain political and religious freedoms, including recognition of four religions: Catholicism, Lutheranism, Calvinism, and Unitarianism. Despite this freedom, however, Catholicism eventually became the strongest religion in Slovakia. Most Catholic parish registers begin in Slovakia in the late seventeenth and early eighteenth centuries.

Protestant churches in Slovakia began sporadically to maintain parish registers in the late sixteenth and early seventeenth centuries. Unfortunately, most of the early church registers from the sixteenth and seventeenth centuries were destroyed as a result of Turkish invasions and Slovak uprisings. Despite such losses, Protestant records generally are better preserved and have more continuity in Slovakia than in the Czech lands because the Hungarian government was more inclined toward Protestantism and buffered the harsh anti-Protestant efforts of the Austrian imperial government. Many Slovak Protestant registers are preserved intact from the early eighteenth century. Samples of several parish registers are shown on the following pages.

The ethnic Ruthene population of Slovakia was Orthodox, using the Slavonic liturgy and ritual. This faith was not recognized by the Habsburg government. To gain legal status and its accompanying freedoms and benefits, these Orthodox Ruthenians agreed in 1649 to recognize the jurisdiction of the pope. The resulting church, in union with the Roman-Catholic church, was called Greek-Catholic. The Greek-Catholic parishes began keeping registers in the mid eighteenth century, and the earliest records are written in Old Church Slavonic and Latin.

Until 1784 church vital records were strictly an ecclesiastical affair, valid only for church purposes. Emperor Josef II recognized the value of vital records for keeping track of

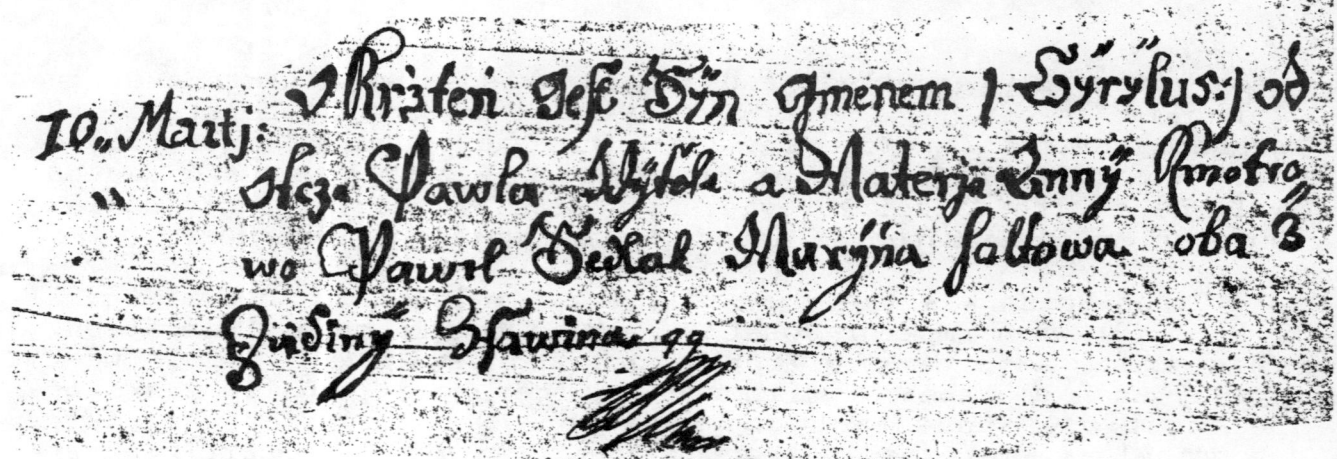

NO. 28. A PARISH REGISTER IN CZECH, 1643 - CHRISTENING.

NO. 29. A PARISH REGISTER IN LATIN, 1678 - MARRIAGES.

This certificate from Slovakia is written in three languages: Latin, Slovak, and Hungarian. The notation at the top indicates that the certificate was made up "for needs in America."

NO. 30. AN EXAMPLE REFLECTING THE DIVERSITY OF LANGUAGES USED IN CZECHOSLOVAKIA.

NO. 31. A JEWISH BIRTH REGISTER IN GERMAN, 1869.

people, especially young men of military age. A law was issued in February 1784 making Catholic registers valid public records. It directed all churches in Austria and Hungary to record births, marriages, and deaths, and made such information the property of the state. This same law required that all registers be kept in German, Hungarian, or Latin. After 1790 it was required that the vital records be indexed, which was done with varying degrees of accuracy. A law was issued in 1799 in the Czech lands, and in 1827 in Hungary, that duplicate copies of vital records be deposited in the bishop's consistory archive. In some areas, such as Moravia, this practice began much earlier. This law is a real boon to researchers today since, in some cases, the original records have been lost or destroyed.

Jewish rabbis were ordered to keep records in 1784, but their books were not considered publicly valid. Early Jewish record keeping was poor at best because of the mobility of the Jewish population and their efforts to avoid conscription. After 1846 the registering of Jewish vital records was made the responsibility of the Catholic clergy, who were to supervise the Jewish books. As a result, the quality of registration improved. This situation continued until 1868 when Jewish registers were declared valid public records.

Civil registration of vital records was introduced in 1869 for persons not recorded in recognized church registers.

After World War I and the formation of the Czechoslovak Republic, a new policy was adopted for the keeping of vital records. In 1920 the registering of births, marriages, and deaths became a purely civil affair; church registers were no longer considered publicly valid. In 1950 the new socialist government declared all church registers to be the property of the state, and in 1952 it began gathering registers more than 100 years old into regional archives. However, a few older records are still in the possession of local records offices [Národní Výbor].

Each archive has an inventory of its vital records holdings. Complete inventories of all available vital records are presently accessible only to the Archival Administration staff in Prague. Most archives have published archival guide books that include inventories of parish registers. These published inventories are quite interesting and valuable because they not only indicate what records are available but usually include a brief history of each parish and information about the villages under the jurisdiction of the parish. These published parish inventories are not available for all of Czechoslovakia, and some were printed before the archive's collection was fully inventoried. Nevertheless, those inventories that are available can be of considerable value to the serious researcher. Fortunately, the LDS Genealogical Library has obtained most of the available published archival guides. For information on these archival guides, see Appendix B.

During World War II nearly all Jewish records in Czechoslovakia were centralized. Those in the Czech lands are presently at the Obvodní Národní Výbor, Matriční Oddělení, in Prague. Jewish records from all of Slovakia were gathered and filed at the Sväz židovských náboženských obcí in Bratislava. These Jewish records, like the Christian registers in regional archives, may be researched through the services of the Archival Administration and the Embassy of the Czechoslovak Socialist Republic in Washington, D.C. (see Chapter 6).

Vital records are the main sources researched when you correspond for genealogical research. Other sources are available; but because of the quality of the vital records, there is seldom any need to refer to them. On those occasions when other sources could and should be consulted, the archival researchers are usually unwilling to do so.

CENSUS RETURNS

The earliest censuses [sčítání lidu] in the Czech lands were simply head counts taken for taxation purposes. It was not until 1651 that the first nominative census was taken; this census counted people by name. It also listed their religion and potential for conversion to the government-sanctioned Catholic church. The rulers wanted to know how many able-bodied men were available for the military or for working the land; the conscription of soldiers was always a concern of the Austrian government. Twice in the eighteenth century, 1754 and 1770, a census was taken to determine potential manpower and to prepare conscription lists. Censuses were taken periodically throughout the nineteenth century for military and taxation purposes. Beginning in 1724 a census of Jews was periodically taken to determine their numbers and influence in the Catholic domains of Austria and Hungary.

Some census returns, including those for the 1651 census, are kept in the archives of the Czechoslovak Ministry of the Interior. Unfortunately, most census returns, which included lists of inhabitants, have been lost. Only a few lists have been preserved in city or district archives. In most cases, only summary information from the censuses is available. Generally, archival researchers rely almost entirely upon vital records [matriky] and usually do not consult census records. If you feel it is necessary, you can specifically request that census records be consulted, but the archival researchers may not comply.

Some census returns have been published, and a limited number are available at the Genealogical Library, notably the 1770 census of Staré Město Praha (the old town of Prague) (943.71/P3 X2p and film no. 873,665).

In Slovakia, censuses were taken in a manner similar to those conducted in the Czech lands, but according to Hungarian law. Some of the Hungarian census returns have been microfilmed in Hungary and are available at the Genealogical Library. It must be emphasized that the census materials at the Genealogical Library pertain only to the former Hungarian territory. These materials are described below:

A. **The 1828 Hungarian Census.** This was a land-and-property census with conscription information. The Genealogical Library has returns for most of the old Hungarian kingdom, including Slovakia and Sub-Carpathian Ruthenia. This census, written in Latin, lists only the names of property owners, with little information about members of the household. Film numbers for this collection can be found in the Genealogical Library Catalog (GLC), which is on microfiche at your branch genealogical library. They are listed under **HUNGARY - CENSUS**.

B. **The 1848 Hungarian Census of Jews.** This census lists name, age, and birthplace for each member of the household. The birthplace information is especially valuable because many of those enumerated had immigrated from other countries. Since few vital records exist for Jews prior to 1846, this census can serve as a substitute.

This Jewish census is available for only part of Hungary. Fortunately, much of what is available covers areas that later became part of Czechoslovakia. Following is a list of film numbers for available records covering Czechoslovak areas. For areas of Hungary not in Czechoslovakia, check the GLC heading **HUNGARY - CENSUS**.

County	Film Number
Esztergom	754,368, item 3 (the same material is found on 719,824, item 3)
Győr	719,824, item 5
Komárom	719,824, item 7
Máramaros	719,825, item 1
Moson	719,825, item 2
Trencsén	719,326, item 1
Turóc	719,368, item 2 (the same material is found on 719,826, item 2)
Ung	719,326, item 3

Many larger cities were enumerated separately from their counties. Incomplete returns for several cities are found on film no. 719,823. Included are the following cities now in Slovakia: Eperjes (now Prešov), Modor (now Modra near Bratislava), Nagy-Szombat (now Trnava), Szakolcza (now Skalica near Nitra), and Trencsén (now Trenčín).

This census is in Hungarian. For some areas, printed forms were used, as shown in illustration no. 32. In other areas, the headings were handwritten versions of the official format, which may vary slightly in wording from the printed version shown. Columns in the example are numbered for convenience in translation. Several counties may be on one film. Counties are filmed alphabetically with the county [megye] name centered at the top of the page. The community name [Közseg neve] is given at the top right. The example shown is for Bes in Ung County, now Beša in Slovakia.

NO. 32. 1848 HUNGARIAN CENSUS OF THE JEWS.

Translation of Headings on the 1848 Hungarian Census of the Jews.

Column 1: Registration number.

Column 2: Name (family members listed in order) [neje - wife; gyermek - children; fia - son; lánya - daughter; szolgáló - servant].

Column 3: Age.

Column 4: Place of birth (a) country, (b) community [Magyar - Hungary; Lengyel - Poland (may include Galicia, Austria); Német - Germany; Orosz - Russia; Porosz - Prussia; Bajor - Bavaria; Cseh - Bohemia; Morva - Moravia; Szilésia - Silesia; Steria - Styria, Steiermark; Gács - Galicia; Románia - Romania; Erdély - Transylvania; Külföldi - foreigner.

Column 5:   If foreigner, does he have a residency permit? [igen - yes; nincs - no].

Column 6:   If he does not have a permit, how long has he lived here? (a) In Hungary. (b) In this community [éve - years; esztendeje - years].

Column 7:   How employed.

Column 8:   Behavior [jó, jól - good; becsületes - honest; jámbor - meek; tűrhéto - bearable; rossz - bad; gyanús - suspicious; csaló - deceitful].

Column 9:   Remarks.

C. <u>The 1857 Hungarian Census</u>. This census enumerated entire households. It indicates all members of the household and shows relationship to the head of the household. It provides data on birth dates, religion, and sometimes place of origin. There are two types of printed forms: one with headings in German and Hungarian, and one with headings in German only. The census is available for only three counties of old Hungary. For Czechoslovakia it is available only for a few towns in Esztergom county as indicated below.

On film no. 720,178, item 2: Béla (now Belá), Bucs (now Búč), Ersekkety (now Kvetná), Farnád (now Farná).

On film no. 720,179: Farnád (continued), Kicsind (now Malá nad Hronom), Muszla (now Mužla), Nagyszölgyin (now Svodín), Párkany (now Šturovo).

These films also include other towns in Esztergom county which are not in Czechoslovakia. For a complete list, check the GLC under the heading **HUNGARY, ESZTERGOM - CENSUS**.

D. <u>The 1869 Hungarian Census</u>. This census gives considerable information on all members of households including birth date and birthplace. Unfortunately, census returns are available only for the old Hungarian county of <u>Zemplén</u> and <u>parts of Esztergom</u> county, most of which are now part of Czechoslovakia. The column headings for this census are in Hungarian. In some cases they also are given in Serbian or in German. An example is given in Appendix C together with a translation of the headings. Appendix C also includes a complete list of all available towns with film numbers.

TAX LISTS

Tax lists [berní ruly] are lists of taxpayers. They were first compiled in 1654. Additional lists were made in 1684, 1746, 1757, and 1792. These lists include only the heads of families who own taxable property or have a trade. They can be quite helpful when an ancestor is known to have been in a taxable status. Tax lists have been deposited in various archives but are not readily accessible to researchers. Some tax lists, however, have been published; and the Genealogical Library has a collection of quite a few volumes (not indexed), all written in Czech. Some volumes include maps showing the various properties. As this book goes to press, these volumes have not yet been microfilmed, but they are available at the Genealogical Library. The call number is 943.7 B4b. When these volumes are microfilmed, you will be able to locate the film numbers in the GLC under the heading CZECHOSLOVAKIA - LAND AND PROPERTY.

LOCAL HISTORIES

Books often are published giving the history of individual towns or cities and vicinity. Such volumes can give valuable insight into the environment in which your ancestors lived. They often include information about the prominent local people who may have played a part in the history of the area. Local histories of a few localities, mostly written in Czech but with some written in German, are available at the Genealogical Library. Consult the library's catalog for the specific locality wanted.

OTHER SOURCES

There are many types of records, if accessible and if used correctly, that can assist the genealogist in building a reliable pedigree of ancestors in Czechoslovakia. Unfortunately, most are not accessible, and extracting information from them may be too time consuming to make them of practical value for researchers. Such records include passport applications, wills and probates, land records, and census records for Czech lands.

Military records for much of the Austro-Hungarian Empire presently are being microfilmed by the Genealogical Library. These records could be of value to researchers, but they are not usable unless the regiment to which the ancestor belonged can be determined from some other source (see illustration no. 33). An index of officers also has been microfilmed; and, since the regiment is not needed to use this index, it could be of considerable value to the few individuals whose ancestors held a position of rank. These records are listed in the GLC under the heading AUSTRIA - MILITARY RECORDS.

The parish registers are the most reliable and complete source of genealogical information. Unless and until the many sources for genealogical research available in Czechoslovakia become readily accessible to researchers in the United States, the Czechoslovak-American genealogists must be satisfied with research that can be done by correspondence--research almost entirely dependent upon parish registers.

NO. 33. AN AUSTRIAN MILITARY RECORD.

CHAPTER 8

LANGUAGES

Perhaps the most difficult aspect of Czechoslovak genealogical research is the multiplicity of languages involved. Record keeping in the lands now included in Czechoslovakia has been conducted in several languages over the years. Many early parish registers in the Czech lands were kept in Czech. After 1620 parishes were required to keep their books in German or Latin. Some books still were maintained in Czech despite the German or Latin language requirement. In many cases this practice was pursued by writing Czech words in Gothic German script. In Slovakia the official language was Hungarian with many registers kept in Latin, German, or Slovak. In a few cases records may have been written in Ukrainian, Old Church Slovanic, Polish, or, in the case of some Jewish records, Yiddish or Hebrew. Many old documents and certificates that surface when searching through family papers will be written in German, Hungarian, or Latin.

Because of the many languages encountered in Czechoslovak records, it is not unusual to see several variations of an ancestor's name depending on the language of the record. An ancestor may appear as **Wenceslaus** in his Latin birth record, as **Wenzel** in his German marriage record, and as **Václav** in the Czech birth records of his children. The same name in Hungarian is **Vencel**. Another example is the Czech name **Vojtěch**; in German it is **Albrecht**; in Latin, **Adalbertus**; in Hungarian, **Béla**. Fortunately, not all names differ so markedly. The Latin **Josephus** is easily recognized as Czech **Josef**, and the Latin **Catharina** as Slovak **Katarina**. A researcher should not be surprised when information is sent from Czechoslovakia with several different appearing names for the same ancestor. A listing of given names with translations in English, Czech, Slovak, Hungarian, Latin, and German is found in Appendix A.

Surnames also are affected by the language in which the record was written. Some priests simply translated the surname into the language of the church register. Czech surnames could be translated into German or vice versa. For example, the Czech surname **Černý** could be translated to **Schwarz**. Similarly, **Nový**, **Novák**, **Novaček**, **Novotný**, and **Novotniček** could be translated into German as **Neumann**. In Slovakia, the Slovak name **Malý** could become **Kis**. Since Latin was used in all areas, it is possible for names to be translated from Czech, Slovak, German, or

Hungarian into Latin. Usually surnames were not translated, but simply altered to fit the spelling and grammar of the language used in the parish register. It is not uncommon to see Czech surnames changed according to German spelling rules. Thus we find Čermák - Tschermak, Šebek - Schebek, Havliček - Hawlitzek. Likewise, German surnames often are seen with Czech spellings: Schultz - Šulc, Schreier - Šrajer, Schmidt - Šmid. In Slovakia a German surname may be seen with a Hungarian spelling: Weiss - Weisz. As discussed in Chapter 1, many immigrants to the United States similarly translated their surnames or altered the spelling to fit English spelling rules. Following is a table of equivalent spellings in Czechoslovak, German, and Hungarian, with their English pronunciation.

Czechoslovak	German	Hungarian	English Pronunciation
aj	ei	aj	b<u>uy</u>
c	z, tz	c, cz	ca<u>ts</u>
č, cz	tsch	cs	<u>ch</u>eap
ď	--	gy	Ru<u>d</u>yard
ě	je	je	<u>y</u>et
ľ	--	ly	mi<u>lli</u>on
ň	--	ny	can<u>y</u>on
ř, rz	--	--	har<u>sh</u>
s	s, ss	sz	<u>s</u>it
š, sz	sch	s	<u>f</u>ish
ť	--	ty	si<u>tu</u>ation
v, w	w	v, w	<u>v</u>ery
ž	(sch)	zs	mea<u>su</u>re

This chapter will include a short discussion of Czechoslovakia's languages and some aids to assist the researcher in reading the materials he may encounter.

Correspondence with the Czechoslovak Embassy may be conducted in English, and the Embassy will reply in English. Reports received from Czechoslovakia, however, will be in Czech or Slovak depending upon where the research is done. Because of this, these languages will be discussed in greater detail.

CZECH AND SLOVAK LANGUAGES

Czechoslovakia has two official languages: Czech and Slovak. Czech is spoken in the Czech lands of Bohemia, Moravia, and Silesia; and Slovak is spoken in Slovakia. The Czech and Slovak languages are very much alike. These two languages developed from the same West Slavonic tongue and are the most similar of all Slavic languages. After 900 A.D. the Czechs and the Slovaks were politically separated for over a thousand years: Slovaks under Hungarian rule, and Czechs dominated by Germanic Austria. Dialectical differences eventually caused the speech of these peoples to develop into separate languages. Although they are very similar, you should be able to tell them apart by the following criteria:

1. Czech has letters ě, ř, and ů which are not found in Slovak.

2. Slovak texts will include the letters ä, ľ, ĺ, ô, and ŕ which are not found in Czech.

3. Slovak has diphthongs (vowel combinations) ia, ie, and iu which are not found in Czech.

Both Czech and Slovak use the Roman alphabet; but by the addition of marks placed above the letters (called diacritic marks), the alphabet can represent all the sounds encountered in these languages. The <u>háček</u> (little hook ˇ) is used over consonants and the letter e to indicate a soft sound. In printed material you will see the <u>apostrof</u> (') used on the letters d, t, and l in place of the <u>háček</u>. The <u>čárka</u> (little line ´) and the <u>kroužek</u> (little circle °) designate a long vowel. Slovak additionally has <u>dve bodky</u> (two little dots ¨) and the <u>vokáň</u> (circumflex ˆ) which indicate vowel changes. These diacritic marks affect alphabetical order. You will have difficulties using dictionaries and gazetteers in Czech or Slovak if you do not take this into account. The alphabetical order for each language is as follows:

CZECH

a á b c č d ď e é ě f g h ch i í j k l m n ň o ó p q r ř s š t ť u ú ů v w x y ý z ž

SLOVAK

a á ä b c č d ď e é f g h ch i í j k l ľ ĺ m n ň o ó ô p q r ŕ s š t ť u ú v w x y ý z ž

The underlined letters are interfiled alphabetically. Some older dictionaries do not separate the r and ř. Note the position of ch after h. The letters q, w, and x are used only in foreign words.

CZECH		SLOVAK	
<u>Letter</u>	<u>Pronunciation</u>	<u>Letter</u>	<u>Pronunciation</u>
a	Arlene	a	Arlene
á	far	á	far
		ä	Adam
b	Betty	b	Betty
c	Lawrence	c	Lawrence
č	Charles	č	Charles

-92-

Czech		Slovak	
d	Doris	d	Doris
ď, d'	Ru**d**yard	ď, d'	Ru**d**yard
e	Ester	e	Ester
é	Claire	é	Claire
ě	yes		
f	Frank	f	Frank
g	Gilbert	g	Gilbert
h	Harold	h	Harold
ch	Loch Ness	ch	Loch Ness
i	Rita	i	Rita
í	Pauline	í	Pauline
j	Yolanda	j	Yolanda
k	Katherine	k	Katherine
l	Luke	l, ĺ	Luke
		ľ, l'	million
m	Mary	m	Mary
n	Nancy	n	Nancy
ň	Tanya	ň	Tanya
o	Otis	o	Otis
ó	coal	ó	coal
		ô	similar to would
p	Paul	p	Paul
r	Pedro	r, ŕ	Pedro
ř	similar to Marsha		
s	Sam	s	Sam
š	Sharon	š	Sharon
t	Terry	t	Terry
ť, t'	Tatyana	ť, t'	Tatyana
u	Rudolf	u	Rudolf
ú, ů	Louis	ú	Louis
v	Victor	v	Victor
y	Sylvia	y	Sylvia
ý	Doreen	ý	Doreen
z	Zelda	z	Zelda
ž	measure	ž	measure

A. <u>Pronunciation</u>. The letter combination **dž** is pronounced in both languages like the **j** in Joyce. The letters **l** and **r** also can serve as vowels, pronounced something like a shortened version of <u>cull</u> and <u>fur</u>. A favorite tongue twister in Czech is "Strc prst skrz krk," a whole sentence without any vowels! It translates as "Stick your finger in your throat," as unpleasant as trying to pronounce it. Slovak also has a long version of the vowels ĺ and ŕ. In some older documents you may find the following:

    cz for č pronounced <u>church</u>
    rz for ř pronounced similar to the sound of Ma<u>rsh</u>a
    sz for š pronounced <u>sh</u>ell
     w for v pronounced <u>v</u>ictory
     j for i pronounced <u>ee</u>l

B. <u>Grammar</u>. In English some words have different endings depending upon how they are used in a sentence. A few examples of this are they-their-them, he-his-him, and who-whose-whom. This changing of words according to grammatical usage is called inflection. Czech and Slovak are Slavic languages and as such are extremely inflective. All nouns and adjectives, including names of people and places, are subject to changes that can be a source of confusion to anyone not familiar with these languages and their complicated grammar.

There are seven cases in the Czech and Slovak languages. That is to say, there are seven sets of noun and adjective endings. These endings depend upon the usage of a word in a sentence or with a particular preposition. There also are three genders: masculine, feminine, and neuter. Gender affects adjectives and past tense verbs. Endings can change depending on the sex or gender of the person or thing being described or performing the action. **Examples:** Narodil se = He was born. Narodila se = She was born. Narodilo se = It (the child) was born.

Grammatically, there are two types of surnames: nouns and adjectives. Surname endings will vary according to the sex of the person.

1. A male surname that ends in a consonant or with a short vowel, -a or -o, is a noun. The female version of such noun surnames will have the ending -ová. **Examples:** Josef Novák, Anna Nováková; Josef Galko, Anna Galková; Josef Procházka, Anna Procházková. When the male version of the surname ends with a consonant preceded by an e, the e is dropped in the female version. **Examples:** Josef Havlíček, Anna Havlíčková; Josef Mladec, Anna Mladcová. An exception is many surnames ending in -el. **Example:** Josef Doležel, Anna Doleželová.

2. A male surname that ends in a long vowel, -ý, is an adjective. The female version of an adjective name will end in -á. **Examples:** Josef Veselý, Anna Veselá; Josef Černý, Anna Černá.

3. A few surnames end in -i or -ů. These are considered nouns but do not change in the female version. **Examples:** Josef Krejčí, Anna Krejčí; Josef Jirků, Anna Jirků.

These names are given here in their standard or nominative form as they should be recorded in your family history. In documents or archival reports, names will have grammatical endings depending on their usage in a sentence.

Male names often will be encountered with the following grammatical endings: -a, -ího, -ého, -e, -emu, -em, -ým, -om. Female surnames are feminized with the basic endings: -ová or -á. Grammatical endings are then added to this base. Female names often are encountered with the endings -y, -u, -i, -é, -ej,

-ou, and -ú. Other endings too numerous to mention also may be found.

Examples:

Syn Josefa Karla Nováka a Anny Flekalové = son of Josef Karel Novák and Anna Flekalová (Flekal).

Dcera Jiřího Havla a Marie Novotné = daughter of Jiří Havel and Marie Novotná.

Kněž pokřtil Jana Tomáše Novotného a Františku Marii Hájkovou = the priest christened Jan Tomáš Novotný and Františka Marie Hájková (Hajek).

Manželství mezi Františkem Jiřím Novým a Katařinou Marii Schmidtovou = marriage between František Jiří Nový and Katarina Marie Schmidtová (Schmidt).

When you encounter a name in inflected form from which you cannot determine the basic form, you should consult someone who speaks the language. Refer, also, to the list of given names in Appendix A.

Place names also are affected by grammar. Place names may be found with the final e deleted or with one of the following endings: -y, -ich, -u, -e, -ě, and others. Some of these endings can affect the base word making it difficult to determine the basic form that would appear on a map. To determine the basic form of a place name, it is best to check the gazetteer of Czechoslovakia, <u>Administratives Gemeindelexikon der Čechoslovakischen Republic</u> (see pages 44-47). Keep in mind that the ending you have often will differ from the name in the gazetteer.

Examples: z Domažlic = from Domažlice, z Prahy = from Praha (Prague), z Plzně - from Plzeň, v Českých Budějovicích = in České Budějovice, v Písku = in Písek, v Praze - in Praha, v Bratislave = in Bratislava, v Prešove = in Prešov, u Vysokého Mýta = at Vysoké Mýto, v Humpolci = in Humpolec.

If you find the language too difficult, you may want to seek help from someone who speaks Czech or Slovak. The LDS Genealogical Library can provide a list of qualified genealogists accredited in Czechoslovak research who can be hired to provide professional assistance. Write to the Genealogical Library, 35 North West Temple Street, Salt Lake City, Utah 84150.

A more thorough explanation of Czech and Slovak grammar can be obtained from textbooks on these languages. For Czech there is <u>Teach Yourself Czech</u> by W. R. and Z. Lee, published by the David McKay Company, in the Hodder and Stroughton <u>Teach Yourself</u> series. This can be obtained by special order at most bookstores. Other textbooks on Czech and Slovak, as well as Czech or Slovak dictionaries, may be more difficult to find, and you will have to work with a bookstore that specializes in Czech and Slovak materials. One company that you may want to contact is listed below.

F. Pancner Inc.
6514 West Cermak Road
Berwyn, Illinois 60402

CZECH WORD LIST

a -- and
bába, babička -- grandmother
bratr -- brother
bydliště -- residence
byl, byli -- was, were
český, -á, -é -- Czech or Bohemian
chalupník -- cottager
chlapec -- boy
církev -- church
č., číslo -- number
datum -- date
dcera -- daughter
děd -- grandfather
den, dne -- day
dítě -- child
dítěte -- of the child
dohoda -- agreement
domkář -- cottager
domovský list -- residency certificate
dvojčata -- twins
evangelický -- protestant
fara -- parish
hospodář -- farmer
jeho -- his
její -- her
jejich -- their
jméno -- name (given)
katolický -- Catholic
kmotři -- godparents
kněz -- priest
kniha -- bock
kovář -- smith
kraj -- county, region
křest -- christening

křestní list -- christening certificate
křtěnec -- the one christened
křtěný, -a -- christened
křtu -- of the christening
kupec -- merchant
let -- years
lože - legitimacy status
malý, -á, -é -- small
manžel -- husband
manželka -- wife
manželský -- legitimate
manželství -- marriage
matka -- mother
matriky -- vital records
měsíc -- month
město -- city
mezi -- between
místo -- place
mládenec -- bachelor
mlynář -- miller
moravský, -á, -é -- Moravian
muž -- man, husband
mužské -- male
naboženství -- religion
narodil se, -a se -- was born
narození -- birth
nemanželský -- illegitimate
neuvedeno -- not mentioned
nevěsta -- bride
obchodník -- merchant

obec -- community
oddací list -- marriage certificate
okres -- district
otec, otce -- father
panna -- maiden
podle -- according to
pohlaví -- sex
pohřeb -- burial
porod -- sex
porodní bába -- midwife
povolání -- occupation
poznámky -- remarks
prarodiče -- grandparents
předek -- ancestor
příčina -- cause
příjmení -- surname
původ -- parentage
ročník -- year (of book)
rodiče -- parents
rodiště -- birthplace
rodný list -- birth certificate
rok -- year
rolník -- farmer (small farm)
roz., rozená -- maiden name
rychtář -- village magistrate
sedlák -- farmer (large farm)
sestra -- sister
slezský, -á, -é -- Silesian (Austrian)
slovenský, -á, -é -- Slovak
smrt -- death
sňatek -- marriage
snoubenec --fiance, betrothed
snoubenka -- fiance, betrothed
sourozenec -- sibling
starý, -á, -é -- old
stav -- marital status
strana -- page, side
svazek -- volume, number
švec -- shoemaker
svědek -- witness
svobodný, -á -- unmarried
svůj, svá, své -- his/her own
syn -- son
tesař -- carpenter
týden -- week
umřel, -a -- died
úmrtí -- death
úmrtní list -- death
uzavření -- contracting (of marriage)
v, ve -- in
vdaná -- married
vdova -- widow
vdovec -- widower
věk -- age
velký, -á, -é -- great, large
ves -- village
výměnkář -- pensioner
výpis -- extract
vyznání -- religion
z, ze -- from, of (a place)
zaměstnání -- occupation
zemědělec -- farmer (small farm)
zemřelý, -á -- deceased
žena -- woman, wife
ženatý -- married
zenich -- bridegroom
ženské -- female
zesnul -- died
židovský -- Jewish

SLOVAK WORD LIST

Most Slovak and Czech terms are the same or quite similar. Following is a list of words that might be encountered which differ significantly from the terms given in the Czech word list.

bol, boli -- was, were
bydlisko -- residence
dedina -- village
deň -- day
dieťata -- of the child
dla -- according to

dňa -- day
ich -- their
krstný list -- christening
    certificate
meno -- name (given)
mesiac -- month
miesto -- place
narodenia -- birth
narodený, -á, -é -- born
predkovia -- ancestors
priezvisko -- surname

ročný, -á -- ... years old
rod -- legitimacy status
rodičia -- parents
rodičov -- of parents
snúbenec -- fiance, betrothed
sobášny list -- marriage
    certificate
súrodenec -- sibling
uzavretia -- contracting
    (of marriage)
zomrel -- died

MONTHS

	Czech	Slovak	English
I.	leden, ledna	január	January
II.	únor, února	február	February
III.	březen, března	marec	March
IV.	duben, dubna	april	April
V.	květen, května	máj	May
VI.	červen, června	jún	June
VII.	červenec, července	júl	July
VIII.	srpen, srpna	august	August
IX.	září	september	September
X	říjen, října	október	October
XI.	listopad, listopadu	november	November
XII.	prosinec, prosince	december	December

DAYS OF THE WEEK

Czech	Slovak	English
neděle	nedeľa	Sunday
pondělí	pondelok	Monday
úterý	utorok	Tuesday
středa	sreda	Wednesday
čtvrtek	štvrtok	Thursday
pátek	piatok	Friday
sobota	sobota	Saturday

NUMBERS

The following list gives Czech numbers; Slovak numbers are quite similar. The list gives two versions of each number: Cardinal/Ordinal. A cardinal number is a counting number: one, two, three.... An ordinal number usually is given in dates: first, second, third....

CARDINAL NUMBERS

	Czech	Slovak
1.	jeden, jedna, jedno	jeden, jedna, jedno
2.	dva, dvě	dva, dve
3.	tři	tri
4.	čtyři	štyri
5.	pět	pät'
6.	šest	šest'
7.	sedm	sedem
8.	osm	osem
9.	devět	devät'
10.	deset	desat'
11.	jedenáct	jedenást'
12.	dvanáct	dvanást'
13.	třináct	trinást'
14.	čtrnáct	štrnast'
15.	patnáct	pätnást'
16.	šestnáct	šestnást'
17.	šedmnáct	sedmnást'
18.	osmnáct	ôsemnást'
19.	devatenáct	devätnast'
20.	dvacet	dvadsat'
21.	dvacet jeden	dvadsat'jeden
22.	dvacet dva	dvadsat'dva
30.	třicet	tridsat'
31.	třicet jeden	tridsat'jeden
40.	čtyřicet	štyridsat
50.	padesát	pät'desiat'
60.	šedesát	sest'desiat'
70.	sedmdesát	sedemdesiat'
80.	osmdesát	osemdesiat'
90.	devadesát	devät'desiat'
100.	sto	sto
200.	dvěstě	dvesto
300.	třista	tristo
400.	čtyřista	štyristo
500.	petset	pät'sto
600.	šestset	seststo
1000.	tisíc	tisíce
1848.	tisíc osmset čtyřicet osm	tisíc ôsemsto štyridsat' ôsem

ORDINAL NUMBERS
(genitive case)

	Czech	Slovak
1st.	prvního	prvého
2nd.	druhého	druhého
3rd.	třetího	tretího

4th.	čtvrtého	štvrtého
5th.	pátého	piateho
6th.	šestého	siesteho
7th.	sedmého	siedmeho
8th.	osmého	ôsmeho
9th.	devátého	deviateho
10th.	desátého	desiateho
11th.	jedenáctého	jedenasteho
12th.	dvanáctého	dvanasteho
20th.	dvacátého	dvadsiateho
21st.	dvacátého prvního	dvadsiateho prvého
22nd.	dvacátého druhého	dvadsiateho druhého
30th.	třicátého	tridsateho
100th.	stého	stého
101st.	sto prvního	sto prvého
200th.	dvoustého	dvojsteho
201st.	dvěstě prvního	dvesto prvého
300th.	třistého	trojstého
400th.	čtyřstého	štvorstého
500th.	pětistého	pätstého
600th.	šestistého	siest'stého
1000th.	tisícího	tisíciho
2000th.	dvoutisícího	dvojtisíciho

DATES

Dates often are written out in full, with ordinal numbers in genitive case, or they may be written in any of the ways shown in the example below:

February 25, 1848

Czech: dvacátého pátého února tisíc osemset čtyřicet osm.
Slovak: dvadsiateho piateho februára tisíc ôsemsto štvridsat' ôsem.

25. unora 1848   25. februára 1848

25. 2. 1848
25. II. 1848

GERMAN LANGUAGE

Many records from the former Austrian parts of Czechoslovakia and some from Slovakia were written in German. German is much more closely related to English than Czech and Slovak, and its grammar does not complicate names and places. Reading German documents, however, is complicated by the fact that they were written in Gothic script. The word list and handwriting guide should assist in basic interpretation of many German documents.

THE GERMAN ALPHABET

GERMAN WORD LIST

Alter -- age
Bezirk -- district
Braut -- bride
Bräutigam -- bridegroom
Dorf -- village
Ehefrau -- wife
ehelich -- legitimate
Eltern -- parents
evangelisch -- evangelical
  Lutheran
Frau -- wife, woman
geboren -- born
Geburt -- birth
Geschlect -- sex
gestorben -- died
getauft -- christened
getraut -- married
Heimatschein -- residency
  certificate
Heirat -- marriage
Jahr -- year
judisch -- Jewish
Jungfrau -- unmarried girl
katolisch -- Catholic
Kind -- child
Kirche -- church
Kopulation -- marriage
ledig -- single

männlich -- male
Matrikel -- register
Monat -- month
Mutter -- mother
Name -- name
Ort -- place
Pfarre -- parish
Schein -- certificate
Sohn -- son
Stadt -- city
Stand -- occupation
starb -- died
sterben -- die
Tag -- day
Taufe -- christening
Tochter -- daughter
Tod -- death
Trauung -- marriage
unehelich -- illegitimate
Urkunde -- document
Vater -- father
verheiratet -- married
verstorben -- deceased
von -- from, of
weiblich -- female
Witwe -- widow
Witwer -- widower

NUMBERS

CARDINALS		ORDINALS	
1.	ein	1st.	erste
2.	zwei	2nd.	zweite
3.	drei	3rd.	dritte
4.	vier	4th.	vierte
5.	fünf	5th.	fünfte
6.	sechs	6th.	sechste
7.	sieben	7th.	siebte, siebente
8.	acht	8th.	achte
9.	neun	9th.	neunte
10.	zehn	10th.	zehnte
11.	elf	11th.	elfte
12.	zwölf	12th.	zwölfte
13.	dreizehn	13th.	dreizehnte
14.	vierzehn	14th.	vierzehnte
15.	fünfzehn	15th.	fünfzehnte
16.	sechzehn	16th.	sechzehnte
17.	siebzehn	17th.	siebzehnte

18.	achtzehn	18th.	achtzehnte
19.	neunzehn	19th.	neunzehnte
20.	zwanzig	20th.	zwanzigste
21.	einundzwanzig	21st.	einundzwanzigste
22.	zweiundzwanzig	22nd.	zweiundzwanzigste
30.	dreißig	30th.	dreißigste
31.	einunddreißig	31st.	einunddreißigste
40.	vierzig	40th.	vierzigste
50.	fünfzig	50th.	fünfzigste
60.	zechzig	60th.	sechzigste
70.	siebzig	70th.	siebzigste
80.	achtzig	80th.	achtzigste
90.	neunzig	90th.	neunzigste
100.	hundert	100th.	hundertste
1000.	tausend	1000th.	tausendste

MONTHS

Januar	Juli
Februar	August
März	September
April	October
Mai	November
Juni	Dezember

LATIN LANGUAGE

Latin was used extensively in all parts of Czechoslovakia. Many documents that may turn up in your home search may be in Latin, especially church certificates of marriage and birth.

Latin also is a highly inflective language but less complex than Czech and Slovak. Common grammatical endings are shown below:

MASCULINE NAMES

Josephus, Joannes -- standard form
Josephi, Joannis -- of Josephus, Joannes
Josephum, Joannem -- direct object

FEMININE NAMES

Anna -- standard form
Annae -- of Anna
Annam -- direct object

LATIN WORD LIST

a -- by, from
aetas -- age
annus -- year
baptizo -- baptize, christen

caelebs -- unmarried man
conjuges -- married couple
copulationis -- of marriage
coram -- in presence of

cum -- with
defunctus, -a -- deceased
dies -- day
domus -- house
ejusdem, eodem -- the same
est -- is
et -- and
ex -- from
filia -- daughter
filius -- son
incola -- inhabitant
infans -- infant
inter -- between
juvenis -- young man
locus -- place
mater, matris -- mother
matrimonium -- marriage
mortuus, -a -- died
natus, -a -- born
nomen -- name
obiit -- died
pagus -- village

parochia -- parish
parentes -- parents
pater, patris -- father
patrini -- godparents
proles -- child
religio -- religion
renatus, -a -- christened
sepultus -- buried
sexus -- sex
sponsa -- bride
sponsus -- groom
spurius -- illegitimate
testimonium -- certificate
testis -- witness
thorus -- legitimacy status
uxor -- wife
vel -- or
vidua -- widow
viduus -- widower
virgo, virginis -- unmarried girl

NUMBERS

CARDINALS

1. unus, -a, -um
2. duo, duae, duo
3. tres, tria
4. quattuor
5. quinque
6. sex
7. septem
8. octo
9. novem
10. decem
11. undecim
12. duodecim
13. tredecim
14. quattuordecim
15. quindecim
16. sedecim
17. septemdecim
18. deuodeviginti
19. undeviginti
20. viginti
21. viginti unus, or unus et viginti
30. triginta

ORDINALS

1st. primus, -a, -um
2nd. secundus (alter)
3rd. tertius
4th. quartus
5th. quintus
6th. sextus
7th. septimus
8th. octavus
9th. nonum
10th. decimus
11th. undecimus
12th. duodecimus
13th. tertius decimus
14th. quartus decimus
15th. quintus decimus
16th. sextus decimus
17th. septimus decimus
18th. duodevigesimus
19th. undevigesimus
20th. vigesimus
21st. vigesimus primus, or unus et vicesimus
30th. trigesimus

HUNGARIAN LANGUAGE

Slovakia was formerly under Hungarian rule; thus, official documents from Slovakia may be written in Hungarian. The available 1869 census of Zemplén County is written in Hungarian with some pages in both Hungarian and Serbian, or Hungarian and German. Many place names given by Slovaks were Hungarian.

Hungarian is a complex language unrelated to Czech or Slovak. It is not even Indo-European, the language family to which almost all other European languages belong. The complex Hungarian grammar adds many endings and prefixes. The following word list gives only basic forms. This list should help in interpreting many documents that you might find relating to your Slovak ancestor. For more detailed needs, you should obtain a Hungarian dictionary. Hungarian numbers are rarely written out in full.

HUNGARIAN WORD LIST

ágostai -- evangelical
állása -- occupation
anya -- mother
anyakönyv -- vital register
apa -- father
asszony -- woman, wife
atya -- father
-ban, -ben -- in
egyház -- church
életkor -- age
és -- and
év -- year
feleség -- wife
férfi -- man, male
férj -- husband
férjezett -- married woman
fi -- male
fia -- son
fiu -- boy
gyerek -- child
hajadon -- single girl
halál -- death
hava -- month
házas -- married
házszam -- house number
hely -- place
hónap --month
ismeretlen -- unknown
izraelita -- Jewish

katholikus -- Catholic
kereszt- -- christening
kis -- little
kor -- age
község -- village
lakhely -- residence
lány -- girl, daughter
legény -- single man
megye -- county
menyasszony -- bride
nagy -- large
nap -- day
neje -- wife
nem -- no, not
neme -- sex
neve -- name
nő -- female
nős -- married man
nőtlen -- single man
özvegy -- widow, widower
református -- reformed
  (Calvinist)
származása -- birthplace
szlovák -- Slovak
születés -- birth
szülők -- parents
temetés -- burial
vallása -- religion
vőlegény -- bridegroom

APPENDIX A. CZECHOSLOVAK GIVEN NAMES.

In the Czech lands and Slovakia, the major source of given names was the names of Roman-Catholic saints. Many of these were borrowed from foreign sources including names of Greek, Latin, Hebrew and German origin.

Other names are of purely Slavic origin. Among these the most popular were compound names which consist of two Slavic roots joined together. The following list gives the meanings of most of the various Slavic prefixes and suffixes.

Prefix Roots

Blaho-	blessed	Lubo-	see Libo-	Zde-	here (or do)
Bohu-	God's	Ludo-	the people	Želi-	desire
Bole-	more	Luti-	fierce	Žito-	life
Bor-	warrior	Milo-	love		
Boži-	see Bohu-	Miro-	peace		Suffix Roots
Brani-	defense	Msti-	revenge		
Breti-	ring out	Radi-	joy	-bor	fight, warrior
Broni-	see Brani-	Rati-	soldier	-chval	praise
Dali-	further, more	Rosti-	increase	-dan	given
Dobro-	good	Slavo-	glory	-dar	gift
Draho-	dear, valued	Sobě-	self	-mil	love
Hori-	mountains	Stani-	everlasting	-mír	peace
Hosti-	guest	Svato-	strong (or Holy)	-mysl	think
Hvězdo-	star	Sveto-	see Svato-	-pluk	defense of people
Jaro-	strong, fierce	Světlo-	light	-rad	joy
Krasno-	beautiful	Vác-	more	-slav	glory
Kraso-	see Krasno-	Vit-	live	-těch	haste
Křeso-	strong	Vladi-	rule	-voj	warrior
Květo-	flower	Vlasti-	homeland	-van	individual
Ladi-	see Vladi-	Voj-	warrior	-vit	life
Libo-	beloved	Vrati-	return		
Lido-	see Ludo-	Zby-	remain		

Thus Vladimír means "rule of peace" and Dalibor means "continue fighting." Of course, not all suffixes are found with all prefixes.

In many cases male names had a female version created by adding -a

Male	Female
Jaroslav	Jaroslava
Bohumil	Bohumila
Vladimír	Vladimíra
František	Františka

Most Czech and Slovak names (of all origins) end in a consonant (František, Jan, etc.) and female names usually end with -a (Kateřina) or -e (Marie). Most names have nicknames or diminutive forms which end in -a, -ek, or ik. For example: Franta from František; Maňa or Mařka from Marie; Jarda or Jarek from Jaroslav, Pavlík from Pavel.

The records in Czechoslovakia were kept in several different languages. The birth record of an individual may have been written in Latin and the marriage record may have been in German or in Hungarian. Usually the given names were translated into the language of the document. In most genealogical reports from Czechoslovakia, names are recorded as they appear in the original documents. This can cause confusion since an ancestor may appear as Vojtěch in one record and Adalbertus in another. The name list given here includes most of the common names found in Czechoslovakia and gives versions in Czech, Slovak, Hungarian, Latin, German and English.

Although this list includes many names; it should be noted that certain names are enormously more common then others. The directory for the city of Prague in 1896 shows that 70% of the male population bore the five most popular names: Josef 22%, František 15%, Václav 12%, Antonín 11%, Jan 10%. Other very popular male names were Karel, Vojtěch, Matěj, Jiří, Alojzy (Alois), Martin and Jakub. The same source indicates that among females 60% bore the five most common names: Marie 22%, Anna 21%, Josefa, 7%, Kateřina 6%, Antonie 4%. Other very popular female names were Františka, Barbora, Terezie and Dorota.

This given-name list, prepared by the author, is used by permission of the Genealogical Library of the Church of Jesus Christ of Latter-day Saints.

MALE NAMES

Czech	Slovak	Hungarian	Latin	German	English
Abraham	Abrahám	Ábrahám	Abraham	Abraham	Abraham
Adam	Adam	Ádám	Adam	Adam	Adam
Adolf	Adolf	Adolf	Adolphus	Adolph	Adolph
Albert (see also Vojtěch)	Albert	Albert	Albertus	Albrecht	Albert
Albín	Albín	Albin or Ölbö	Albinus	Albín	Albin
Alojzy	Alojz	Alajos	Aloisius	Alois	Aloysius or Louis
Ambrož	Ambróz	Ambrus or Ambrö	Ambrosius	Ambrosius	Ambrose
Andřej or Ondřej	Andrej or Ondrej	András or Endre	Andreas	Andreas	Andrew
Antonín	Anton	Antos or Antal	Antonius	Anton	Anthony
Arnošt	Ernest	Ernö	Ernestus	Ernst	Ernest
Artur	Artúr	Artur	Arthur	Arthur	Arthur
August	August	Ágost	Augustus	August	August
Baltazar	Baltazár	Baltazár or Baldizsár	Balthassar	Balthasar	Balthasar
Baptista or Křtitel	Baptista or Krstitel	Baptista or Keresztelo	Baptista	Baptist	Baptist
Bartoloměj	Bartolomej	Bartos or Bertalan	Bartholomaeus	Bartholomäus	Bartholomew
				(see Vasil)	Basil
Bedřich	Bedrich	Frigyes	Fredericus	Fridrich or Frederik	Fredrick
Blahomír	Blahomír				
Blažej	Blažej	Balazs	Blasius	Blasius	(none)
Bohdan	Bohdan	Adeodát	Deodatus	Deodat	Theodore
Bohumil or Bohuš (see also Teofil)	Bohumil	Gotlíb	Amadeus or Bohumilus	Gottlieb	Theophil or none
Bohumír	Bohumír	Gotfrid	Godefredus or Gottfridus	Gottfried	Godfrey
Bohuš	(see Bohumil)				
Bohuslav	Bohuslav		Bohuslaus	Botthold	(none)
Boleslav	Boleslav	Boleszló	Boleslaus or Botthold	Boleslaw	Boleslas
Bořivoj	Borivoj				
Bronislav	Branislav				
				(see Karel)	Charles
Česlav	Česlav	Csaszló	Ceslaus	Ceslaus	Ceslas

-107-

MALE NAMES

Czech	Slovak	Hungarian	Latin	German	English
Ctibor	Ctibor				
Cyprián	Cyprián	Ciprián	Cyprianus	Cyprian	Cyprian
Cyril	Cyril	Cirill	Cyrillus	Cyrill	Cyril
Daniel	Daniel	Danylo	Daniel	Daniel	Daniel
Denis	Dionyz or Denis	Denes or Gyenes	Dionysius	Dionys	Dennis
Dětřich	Teodorik	Detre	Theodoricus	Diedrich	Derek
Dionysius	Dyonyz	Dénes or Gyenes	Dionysius	Dionysius	Dennis
Dobromil	Dobromil				
Dušan	Dušan				
Eduard	Eduard	Edvárd	Eduardus	Eduard	Edward
Egid or Jiljí	Egid	Egyed	Aegidius	Ägidius	Giles
Emerich	Imrich	Imre	Americus	Emerich	Emery
Emil	Emil	Emil	Aemilius	Emil	Emil
				See Arnošt	Ernest
Evžen or Eugen	Eugen	Jenő or Eugén	Eugenius	Eugen	Eugene
František	František	Ferenc	Franciscus	Franz	Frank
				(see Bedřich)	Fredrich
Gregor	(see Řehor)				
				(see Jindřich)	Henry
Honza	(see Jan)				
Heřman	Herman	Armand	Hermannus	Hermann	Herman
Ignác	Ignác or Vatroslav	Ignac	Ignatius	Ignaz	Ignatius
Ivan (see also Jan)	Ivan	Ivan	Joannes or Johannes	Johann	John
Jachým	Joachim	Joakim	Joachim	Joachim	Joachim
Jakub	Jakub	Jakab	Jacobus	Jakob	Jacob or James
Jan (see also Ivan)	Jan	János	Joannes or Johannes	Johannes	John
Jaromil					
Jaroslav	Jaroslav				
Jeroným	Hieronym	Jeromos	Hieronymus	Hieronymus	Jerome
Jiljí (see Egid)					

MALE NAMES

Czech	Slovak	Hungarian	Latin	German	English
Jindřich or Hynek	Henrik	Henrik	Henricus	Heinrich	Henry
Jiří	Juraj	György	Georgius	Georg	George
Josef	Jozef	József	Josephus	Joseph	Joseph
Kajetán	Kajetan	Kajetán	Cajetanus	Kajetan	Cajetan
Karel	Karol	Károly	Carolus	Karl	Charles
Kašpar	Gašpar	Gaspar	Casparus	Kaspar	Casper
Kristián	Kristián	Kerestély or Krisztian	Christianus	Christian	Christian
Křtitel (see Baptista)					
Kryštof	Krištof	Kristóf	Christophorus	Christoph	Christofer
Ladislav	(see Vladislav)				
				(see Vavřinec)	Lawrence
Leo, Lev or Leoš	Leo or Lev	Leo	Leo	Leo	Leo or Leon
Libor	Lubor				
Ludvík or Ludovit	L'udovit (see also Alojzy)	Ludovicus	Ludwig		Louis
Lukaš	Lukas	Lukács	Lucas or Lucius	Lukas	Luke
Marcel	Marcel	Marcell	Marcellus	Marcellus	Marcel
Marek	Marek	Márk	Marcus	Markus or Mark	Mark
Martin	Martin	Martón	Martinus	Martin	Martin
Matěj or Matyaš	Matej	Mátyás	Matthias	Matthias	Matthias
Matouš	Matúš	Máté	Matthaeus	Mattäus	Matthew
Metoděj	Metod	Metód	Methodius	Methodius	Methodius
Michal	Michal	Mihály	Michael	Michael	Michael
Mikuláš	Mikuláš	Miklós	Nicholaus	Niklaus	Nicholas
Miloš	Miloš				
Miroslav	Miroslav	Mirkó	Miroslaus		
Mořic	Moríc	Móric	Mauritius	Moritz	Morris or Maurice
Mstislav					
Nepomuk	Nepomuk	Nepomuk	Nepomucenus	Nepomuk	Nepomucene
Oldřich	Oldrich or Ulrich	Ulrik	Ulricus	Ulrich	Ulrick

-109-

MALE NAMES

Czech	Slovak	Hungarian	Latin	German	English
Ondřej (see Andřej)					
Onufry	Onufer	Onufer	Onuphrius	Onuphrius	Humphrey
Pankrác	Pankrác	Pongrác	Pancratius	Pankraz	(none)
Pavel	Pavol	Pál	Paulus	Paul	Paul
Petr	Peter	Péter or Pető	Petrus	Peter	Peter
Prokop	Prokop	Prokop	Procopius	Prokop	Procop
Řehoř	Gregor	Gergely or Gergő	Gregorius	Gregor	Gregory
Rostislav					
Šebestian	Šebastian	Sebestyén or Sebő	Sebastianus	Sebastian or Bastian	Sebastian
Sergej	Sergej	Szergiusz	Sergius	Sergius	Serge
Servác	Servác	Szervác	Servatius	Servatius	(none)
Severin	Severin	Szörény or Szeverin	Severinus	Severin	Severin
Sigfrid	Sigfríd	Szigfrid or Szeveréd	Sigfridus	Siegfried	Sigfried
				Zikmund	Sigmund
Simon	Simon	Simon	Simon	Simon	Simon
Slavomír					
Stanislav	Stanislav	Szaniszló	Stanislaus	Stanislaus or Stenzel	Stanley
Štěpan	Stefan	Istvan or Csépán	Stephanus	Stefan	Steven
				(see Zdeněk)	Sydney
Svatopluk					
Tadeáš	Tadeáš	Tádé	Thaddaeus	Thaddäus or Thadeus	Thaddeus
Teodor (see also Bohdan)	Teodor or Fedor	Tivador or Tódor	Theodorus	Theodor	Theodore
Teofil (see also Bohumil)	Teofil	Teofil	Theophilus	Theophil	Theophil
Timotěj	Timotej	Timót	Timotheus	Timotheus	Timothy
Tomáš	Tomaš	Tamás	Thomas	Thomas	Thomas
				(see Oldřich)	Ulrick
Urban	Urban	Orbán	Urbanus	Urban	Urban
Václav	Václav	Vencel	Venceslaus	Wenzel or Wenzeslaus	(none)

-110-

MALE NAMES

Czech	Slovak	Hungarian	Latin	German	English
Valentin or Valentýn	Valentin	Bálint or Valentin	Valentinus	Valentin	Valentine
Valtr	Valter	Valter	Gualterus	Walter	Walter
Vasil	Bazil or Vasil	Bazil or Vaszoly	Basilius		Basil
Vavřinec	Vavrinec	Lőrince	Laurentius	Lorenz	Lawrence
Viktor	Viktor	Győző or Viktor	Victor	Viktor	Victor
Vilém	Viliam	Vilmos	Guilielmus	Wilhelm	Willi
Vincenc or Čehek	Vincent	Vince or Bence	Vincentius	Vincenz	Vincent
Vít	Vít	Vitus or Vidos	Vitus	Veit or Vitus	Guy
Vladimír	Vladimír	Ladomér	Vladimirus	Wladimir	(none)
Vladislav or Ladislav	Vladislav or Ladislav	László	Ladislaus	Wladislaw	(none)
Vlastislav					
Vojtěch	Vojtech	Adalbert or Béla	Adalbertus	Adelbert	Adelbert or Albert
Volfgang	Volfgang	Farkas	Wolfgangus	Wolfgang	Wolfgang
Vuk	Vlk	Farkas	Lupus	Wolf	Wolfe
Zdeněk	Zdenko	Szidón	Sidonius	Sidonius	Sidney
Zigmund or Zikmund	Zigmund or Zigmund	Zsigmund	Sigismund	Siegmund	Sigmund

FEMALE NAMES

Czech	Slovak	Hungarian	Latin	German	English
Agáta	Agáta	Agota	Agatha	Agathe	Agatha
Albína or Běla	Albína	Albina	Albina	Albina	Albina
Aloisie	Alojzia	Alojzia	Aloisia	Aloisia	Aloysia
Alžběta	Alžbeta	Erzsébet	Elisabetha	Elisabetha	Elizabeth
Amálie	Amalia	Amalia	Amalia	Amelie	Amelia
Anděla	Andela	Angéla	Angela	Angela	Angela
Anna	Anna	Anna	Anna	Anne	Ann
Anežka	Agnesa	Agnes	Agnes	Agnes	Agnes
Antonie	Antonia	Antónia or Ténia	Antonia	Antonie	Antonia
Apolónie	Apolónia	Apolya	Apollonia	Apollonia	Apollonia
Barbora	Barbora	Barbála	Barbara	Barbara	Barbara
Bedřiška	Frederika	Friderika	Friderica	Frederike	Frederica
Bibiana	Bibiána	Bibiana	Viviana	Viviana	Vivian
Blahomila	Blahomila		Blahomila		
Blanka	Blanka	Blanka	Blanka	Blanka	Blanche
Blažena	Blažena		Blasia	Blasia	Blasia
Bohumila	Bohumila		Bohumila	Gottliebe or Godelieva	
Bohdana	Bohdana	Dea	Deodata or Theodora	Deodata or Theodora	Theodora or Godiva
Božena or Beatrice	Božena or Beatrica	Bolda or Beatrix	Beatrix or Beatricia	Beatrice or Theone	Beatrice
Bronislava	Bronislava		Bronislava	Bronislawa	Bronislava
Dobromila					
Dorota	Dorota	Dorottya	Dorothea	Dorothea	Dorothy
Edita	Edita	Edit	Editha	Editha	Edith
Eliška	Eliška or Liza	Eliza or Elza	Elisa	Elise	Elsie
				see Alžběta	Elisabeth
Emilie	Emilia	Emilia	Aemilia	Emilie	Emily
Flora or Květa	Flora or Kveta	Virag	Flora	Flore	Flora
Františka	Františka	Ferike or Franciska	Francisca	Franziska	Frances
				(see Bedřiška)	Frederica
Gertruda	Gertrúda	Gertrúd	Gertrudis	Gertrude	Gertrude

FEMALE NAMES

Czech	Slovak	Hungarian	Latin	German	English
Hana or Ivana	Hana or Ivana	Hanna	Joanna	Johanne or Hana	Hanna or Joan
Hedvika	Hedviga	Hedda or Hedvig	Hedvigis	Hedwig	Avis
Hermína	Hermína	Hermina	Hermina	Hermine	Hermine
Ivana (see Hana)					
Jana (see Hana)					
Jarmila	Jarmila				
Jindřiška	Henrika	Henrietta	Henrica	Hendrike or Henriette	Henrietta
Jiřina	Jirina or Jurajka	Györgyi	Georgia	Georgia	Georgia
Jitka	Judita	Judit	Juditha	Juditha	Judith
Josefa	Jozefa	Józsa or Jozefa	Josepha	Josepha or Josephina	Josephine
Julie	Julia	Júlia	Julia	Julia	Julia
Kateřina	Katerina	Katalin	Catharina	Katharine	Catherine
Kunhuta or Kunigunda	Kunhuta or Kunigunda	Kinga or Gunda	Cunegundis	Kunigunda or Kynga	
Květa (see Flora)					
Květoslava					
Liběna	Lubica	Karitász	Caritas	Caritas	Charity
Libuše	Libuša	Libusa	Libussa	Libussa	
Lucie	Lucie	Lúcia	Lucia	Lucia	Lucy
Ludmila	Ľudmila	Ludmilla	Lidmila	Lidmilla	Ludmilla
Lujza	Lujza				
Magdaléna	Magdaléna	Madlena	Magdalena	Magdalena	Madeline
Marcéla	Marcela	Marcella	Marcella	Marcella	Marcella
Marie	Maria	Maria	Maria	Marie	Mary
Markéta	Margita	Margó	Margarita	Margrethe	Margaret
Marta	Marta	Márta	Martha	Martha	Martha
Oldřiska	Ulrika	Ulrika	Ulrica	Urike	Ulrica
Pavla	Pavla or Paula	Paula	Paula	Pauline	Paula or Pauline
Renáta	Renáta	Renáta	Renata	Renate	Renata
Rozálie	Rozálie	Rozalie	Rosalia	Rosalie	Rosalie

FEMALE NAMES

Czech	Slovak	Hungarian	Latin	German	English
Rút	Rút	Ruth	Ruth	Ruth	Ruth
Ružena	Ružena or Ruža	Rozsa or Rozina	Rosa	Rosina or Rosa	Rose
Sofie (see Žofie)					
Stanislava	Stanislava		Stanislava		
Štěpanka	Štefania	Istvánka	Stephana	Stefanie	Stephanie
Svata					
Světla (see Lucie)					
				(see Zdenka)	Sidonia
				(see Zuzana)	Susan
Taťána	Taťána	Tatjána	Tatiana	Tatiana	Tatiana
Tekla	Tekla	Tekla	Thecla	Thekla	(none)
Terezie	Terezia	Teréz	Teresia	Therese	Teresa
Uršula or Voršila	Uršula	Orsolya or Orsika	Ursula	Ursula	Ursula
Vaclava	Vaclava				
Věra	Viera	Fidesz	Fidelia	Vera.	Vera or Faith
Veronika	Veronika	Veronika	Veronica	Veronika	Veronica or Bernice
Viktoria	Viktoria	Viktoria	Victoria	Viktoria	Victoria
Vlasta	Vlasta				
Xénie	Xénie		Xenia	Xenia	Xenia
Zdenka	Zdenka	Zsidónia	Sidonia	Sidonie	Sidonia
Žofie	Žofie	Zsófia	Sophia	Sofie	Sophia
Zuzana	Suzana	Zsuzsanna	Susanna	Susanna	Susan

APPENDIX B. PARISH INVENTORIES.

Most vital records [matriky] and other genealogical sources are deposited in State Regional Archives [Státní oblastní archivy]. Many of the State Regional Archives and branch State Regional Archives that have vital records in their collections have published parish inventories. These parish inventories list the specific records available for each parish. They also include information on the history of the parish, its parent parish, if any, etc. This information can be helpful in making specific requests for genealogical research.

The LDS Genealogical Library has obtained published parish inventories for most of Czechoslovakia. Some were published before the archive concerned had fully inventoried its holdings and are, thus, incomplete. The map on page 115 shows which archives have published parish inventories for the areas as indicated. The list below gives details about the publication for that archive.

PARISH INVENTORIES AVAILABLE

Archive	Year Published	Pages	Book Call Number	Film Number
Banská Bystrica			See note below.	
Bratislava			See note below.	
Brno město (city)	1956	116-119	943.7 A3a, part 1	1,181,592, item 4
Bytča			See note below.	
Jablonec	1956	89-124	943.71/J2 A3sa	908,258, item 2
Janovice	1957	104-125	943.72/J1 A3sa	1,181,587, item 4
Košice			See note below.	
Litoměřice	1956	156-208	943.71/L2 A3sa, V. 1	1,181,587, item 3
Nitra			See note below.	
Opava*	1955	95- 97	943.72/O1 A3sa, V. 1	1,181,587, item 1
Plzeň	1958	128-173	943.71/P2 A3sa	962,395, item 2
Praha	1958	233-312	943.71/P3 A3sa, V. 1	962,466, item 2
Praha město (city)	1954	12- 25	943.71/P3 K23h	908,084, item 2
Prešov			See note below.	
Třeboň	1957	159-208	943.71/T2 A3sa	1,181.587, item 2
Zámrsk	1965	183-261	943.71/Z1 A3sa	1,181,589, item 1

*Not fully inventoried.

NOTE: A complete inventory of vital records in Slovak archives has recently been published. This is <u>Prehľad matrík na Slovensku do zoštatnenia matričnej agendy</u> [Survey of vital records in Slovakia up to the beginning of civil registration] by Jana Kalesná (Bratislava: Archívna správa ministerstva vnútra SSR, 1982). It is available through the Genealogical Library. The call number is 943.73 K23k (film no. 1,183,541, item 4, or microfiche no. 6,000,786). Similar works for Bohemia and Moravia also may be published and will be acquired by the Genealogical Library if they become available.

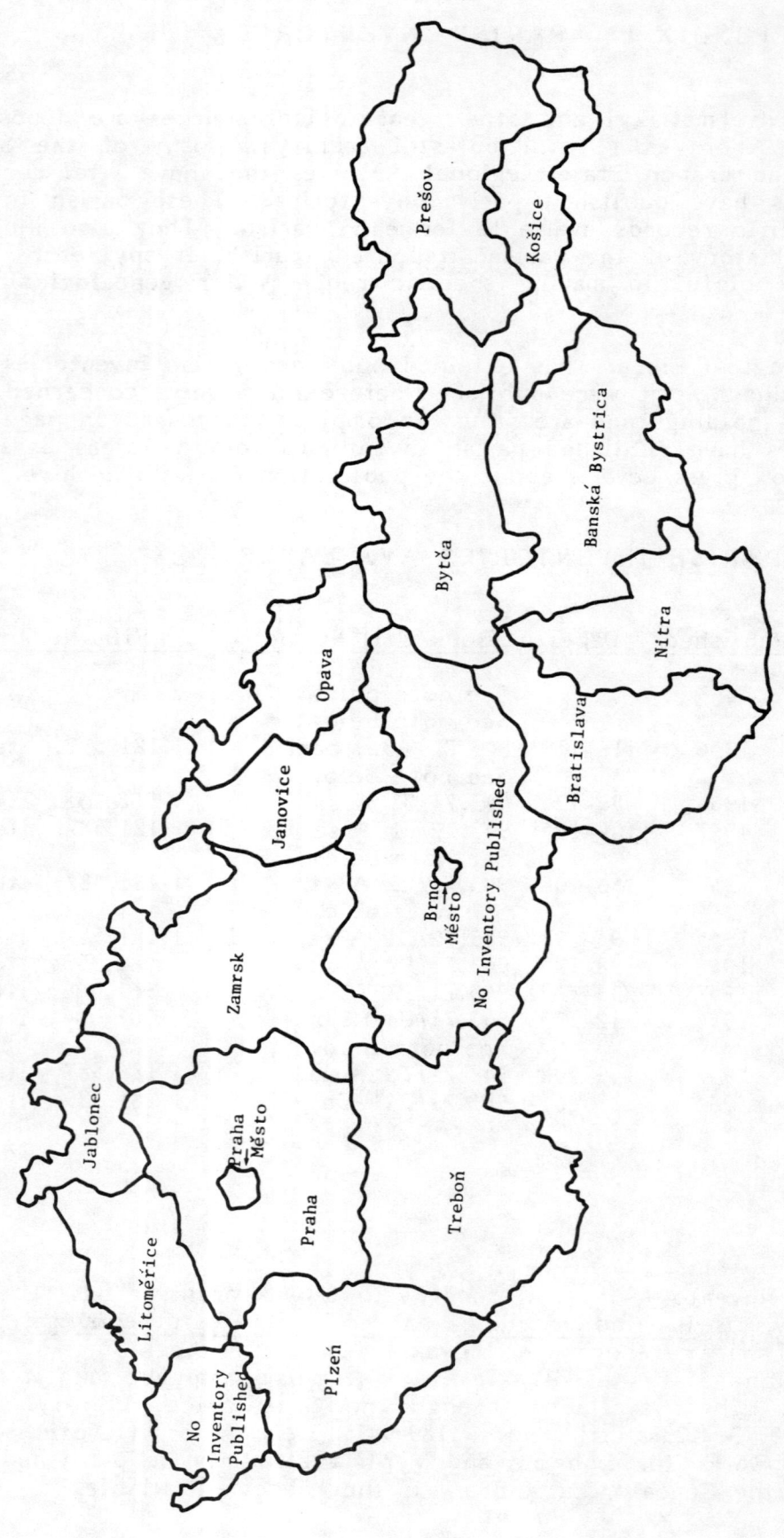

NO. 34. ARCHIVAL DISTRICTS FOR WHICH INVENTORIES HAVE BEEN PUBLISHED.

APPENDIX C. MICROFILM NUMBERS FOR THE 1869 CENSUS OF ZEMPLÉN AND PART OF ESZTERGOM COUNTY.

This appendix lists localities in Zemplén and Esztergom counties according to the standard Hungarian spelling as found in the old 1880 Hungarian gazetteer, Magyarország Helységnévtára (Ref. 943.9 E5d; Vol. I on film no. 599,564, Vol. II on film no. 973,041). Localities on this list are in Zemplén county unless otherwise indicated. You will note that some localities in Zemplén county are noted as being in Saros county. This is because of slight shifting in county borders between the time of the 1869 census and the 1880 gazetteer.

Many of these localities have been known by several additional names, especially those localities that are now in Czechoslovakia. If you have only the Czechoslovak place name or, perhaps, a German or alternate Hungarian version, it will not appear on this list. For localities in Czechoslovakia, an excellent gazetteer is available listing all variant place names for all localities in Slovakia. This is Názvy obcí na Slovensku za ostatných dvesto rokov (Ref. 943. 73 E2m; film no. 1,181,569, item 1). Instructions for using this gazetteer are given in English on the flyleaf of the book. The Hungarian spelling used in this appendix usually corresponds with the spelling that Názvy obcí indicates with the date 1863. Eventually all localities in Czechoslovakia will be cataloged under their Czechoslovak names in the computer catalog, available on microfiche at branch libraries. A somewhat less accurate cataloging by Czechoslovak place names is already available under Czechoslovakia, Vychodoslovensky kraj (film no. 934,411).

An example of the 1869 Hungarian census is shown in illustration no. 35. Column headings are in Hungarian. In some cases, they also are given in Serbian or in German.

TRANSLATION OF HEADINGS ON THE 1869 HUNGARIAN CENSUS

Column 0: Consecutive number of residence.

Column 1: Consecutive number of individual.

Column 2: Surname, given name, title, and rank of the resident.
To be recorded in the following order: (1) head of household, (2) wife, (3) child, grandchildren according to age, (4) relatives, (5) guests, servants, apprentices, etc., (6) roomer and lodgers.

Column 3: Sex [férfi - male; nő - female].

Column 4: Year of birth.

Column 5: Religion [római-kathólikus - Roman-Catholic; görög-kathólikus - Greek-Catholic; örmény-kathólikus - Armenian-Catholic; keleti egyházbeli - Orthodox; helvét-evangelikus - Swiss Evangelical, Reformed; ágostai-evangélikus - Augsburg Evangelical; unitárus - Unitarian; mózes - Jewish].

NO. 35. 1869 HUNGARIAN CENSUS.

Column 6: Marital status [nőtlen - single male; hajadon - single female; házas - married; nős - married man; férjezett - married woman; özvegy - widow, widower; elvált - divorced].

Column 7: Occupation or ....

Column 8: Profession.

Column 9: Birthplace (country, county, town).

Column 10: Citizenship [helybeli - native; idegen - foreigner].

Column 12: Absence [innen ideiglen - temporary; túl huzamosan - prolonged].

Column 13: Literacy [olvasni - reading; írni - writing; tud - knows how; nem tud - doesn't know how].

Column 14: Remarks.

LIST OF MICROFILM NUMBERS

Locality	Film number	Item on film
ABARA	722,666	
AGÁRD	722,667	
AGYAGOS	722,668	1
AGYIDÓCZ	766,668	2
ALSÓ- (prefix meaning "lower" / See place name without prefix)		
ARANYOSPATAK	722,670	4
ARDÓ (VÉG-)	722,671	1
ARDONYA (BODROG-)	See ZSADÁNY	
ARDONYA-ZSADÁNY	See ZSADÁNY	
AZAR (KIS-)	722,718	1
AZAR (NAGY-)	722,749	
BACSKA	722,671	2
BACSKÓ	722,671	3
BAJÓTH, Esztergom county	720,180	2
BÁNYÁCZKA (BUDA-)	719,777	1 labeled as RUDABÁNYÁCSKA
BÁNYÁCSKA (KIS-)	722,718	2
BANÓCZ	722,672	4
BÁNSZKA	722,673	1
BARANCS	722,672	1
BÁRI (KIS-)	722,718	3
BÁRI (NAGY-)	722,749	2
BARKÓ	722,672	2
BASKOCZ	722,672	3
BATTYÁN	722,679	3 labeled as BOTTYÁN
BEKECS	722,673	2

BÉLA, Esztergom county	720,181	1
BÉLA (CZIROKA-)	722,682	
BÉLA (IZBUGYA-) and VALENTOCZ	722,711	1
BÉLY	722,674	3 labeled as BÉLLY
BENYE (LEGYES-)	722,733	
BERECZKI (ALSÓ-)	722,668	3
BERECZKI (FELSŐ-)	722,694	3
BERETTŐ	722,674	1
BERZÉK	722,674	2
BISTE	722,675	1
BISZTRA (OROSZ-)	722,760	4
BISZTRA (TAPOLY-), Saros county	720,011	2 labeled as TÓT-BISZTRA
BÓCS (KÜLSŐ-)	722,718	4 labeled as KIS-BÓCS
BODROG- (prefix / See place name without prefix)		
BODZÁS	722,677	4
BODZÁS-UJLAK	See UJLAK (BODZÁS-NAGY-)	
BOLY	722,678	2 labeled as BOLLY
BORRÓ	722,678	3
BORSI	722,679	1
BOSNYICZA	722,679	2
BOTTYÁN	See BATTYÁN	
BRESNYICZE (KIS-)	722,718	5
BRESNYICZE (NAGY-)	722,749	3
BRESZTÓ (HOMONNA-)	722,679	4
BRESZTÓ (IZBUGYA-)	722,711	2
BREZÓCZ	See BREZOVECZ	
BREZOVECZ	722,680	1 labeled as BREZÓCZ
BRUSNYICZA	722,680	2
BUDA-BÁNYÁCZKA	See BÁNYÁCZKA (BUDA-)	
BUKÓCZ	722,680	3
BUTKA	722,680	4
CÉKE	See CZÉKE	
CIGÁND	See CZIGÁND	
CIROKA	See CZIROKA	
CSABALÓCZ-SZTERKÓCZ	722,683	2 labeled as CSABALÓCS
CSABALÓCZ-SZTERKÓCZ	719,794	1 labeled as SZTERKÓCZ
CSÁKLYÓ	722,684	1
CSASANÁLOS (UJ-)	720,016	2
CSEBB (KIS- and NAGY-)	722,750	2
CSEBINYE (ALSÓ-)	722,668	4
CSEBINYE (FELSŐ-)	722,694	4
CSEBINYE (HORBOK-)	722,709	2 labeled as HARBOK-CSEBINYE
CSÉCS (KIS-)	722,720	1
CSÉKE	722,685	2
CSELEJ	722,684	2

CSEMERNYE (MÁRK-)	See MARK-CSEMERNYE	
CSEMERNYE (VARANNÓ-)	720,019	1
CSERNAHÓ	722,684	3
CSERTÉSZ	722,685	1
CSICSÓKA	722,685	3
CSICSVAALJA (PUSZTA-)	722,685	4
CSOLNOK, Esztergom county	720,181	2
CSORGÓ	722,685	5
CSUKALÓCZ	722,685	6
CZABÓCZ	722,681	1 labeled as CSABÓCZ
CZÉKE	722,681	2
CSERNYINA	722,684	4
CZIGÁND (KIS-)	722,719	
CZIGÁND (NAGY-)	722,750	1
CZIROKA- (prefix / See place name without prefix)		
DÁGH, Esztergom county	720,181	3
DAMÓCZ	722686	3
DARA	722,686	1
DARGÓ	722,686	2
DÁVIDVÁGÁS	722,686	4
DEDASÓCZ	722,687	1
DEREGNYŐ	722,687	3
DETRIK	722,687	2
DOBRA (KIS-)	722,688	1
DOBRA (NAGY-)	719,802	3 labeled as ZEMPLÉN-DOBRA
DOBRA (ZEMPLÉN-)	See DOBRA (NAGY-)	
DOBSZA (KIS-)	722,720	2
DOMÁSA (KIS-)	722,720	3
DOMÁSA (NAGY-)	722,751	1
DRICSNA	722,688	2
DÚBRAVA	722,688	3 labeled as DÚBRA
DUBRÓKA	722,688	4
EGRES	722,689	
ERDŐ-BENYE	See BENYE (ERDŐ-)	
ERDŐ-HORVÁTI	See HORVÁTI (ERDŐ-)	
FALKUS	722,694	1
FEKETEPATAK	722,694	2
FELSŐ- (prefix meaning "upper" / See place name without prefix)		
FIAS, Saros county	722,695	6
FÜZESÉR	722,695	7
GÁLSZÉCS	722,697	
	722,698	
GARANY	722,696	1
GATÁLY	722,696	2
GERCSELY	722,699	1
GERENDA	722,699	2
GÉRES (KIS-)	722,720	4

GÉRES (NAGY-)	722,751	2
GESZTELY		
GIGLÓCZ	722,701	1
GIRINCS	722,701	2
GIRÓCZ	722,701	3
GOLOP (ALSÓ-)	722,668	5
GOLOP (FELSŐ-)	722,694	5
GÖRÖGINYE	722,701	4
GROZÓCZ	722,701	5
GYAPALÓCZ	722,701	6
GYÖRGYÖS, Sáros county	722,701	7
HABURA	722,702	1
HANKÓCZ	722,702	2
HARDICSA	722,702	3
HARKÁNY	722,797	2 labeled as TAKTA-HARKANY
HAVAJ	722,703	1
HAZSINA	722,703	2
HEGEDÜSFALVA	722,703	3
HEGYI	722,703	4
HELMECZ (KIRÁLY-)	722,717	
HELMECZKE	722,704	1
HENCZÓCZ	722,704	2
HERMANY (TAPOLY-ZEMPLÉN-), Sáros county	720,000	2
HERNÁD-KAK	See KAK (HERNÁD-)	
HERNÁD-NEMETI	See NEMETI (HERNÁD-)	
HIDVÉG (SAJÓ-)	719,778	1
HOCSA	722,706	1
HOLCSIKÓCZ	722,706	2 labeled as HOLYCSILÓCZ
HOMONNA	722,707	
HOMONNA- (prefix / See place name without prefix)		
HOPORTY	See SÓSTÓFALU	
HOÓR	722,708	4
HORBOK- (prefix / See place name without prefix)		
HORVATI (ERDŐ-)	722,693	
HOSSZULÁZ	722,709	5
HOSSZUMEZŐ (CZIROKA-)	722,683	1
HUSSZUMEZŐ (IZBUGYA-)	722,711	3
HOSSZUMEZŐ (KOLCS-)	722,725	1
HOSSZUMEZO (VARANNÓ-)	720,019	2
HOSZTOVICZA	722,709	4
HOTYKA (MAKKOS-)	722,738	4
HRABÓCZ (ALSÓ-)	722,669	1
HRABÓCZ (IZBUGYA-)	722,711	4
HRABÓCZ (OROSZ-)	722,760	5
HRUBÓ	722,709	6
IMREG	722,710	1
INÓCZ	722,710	2
ISZTÁNCS	722,710	3
IZBUGYA	722,710	4
IZBUGYA- (prefix / See place name without prefix)		

IZSÉP (TAPOLY-)	720,011	3 labeled as TÓTH-IZSÉP
IZSÉP (TÓT-)	See IZSÉP (TAPOLY-)	
JABLONKA (ALSÓ-)	722,669	2
JABLONKA (FELSŐ-)	722,695	1
JABLONYA (TÓT-)	720,011	4
JAKUSÓCZ	722,712	1 labeled as JAKASOCZ
JALOVA	722,712	2
JANKÓCZ	722,712	3
JESZENŐCZ	722,712	4
JESZENŐ	722,712	5
JESZTREB (MAGYAR-)	722,737	2
JESZTREB (TÓT-)	720,012	1
JÓZSEFFALVA	722,712	6
JÓZSEFVOLGY	722,712	7
JUSZKO-VOLYA	See VOLYA (JUSZKO-)	
KÁCSÁND	722,714	5
KAJNYA (OROSZ-)	722,761	1
KAJNYA (TÓT-)	720,012	2
KAK (HERNÁD-)	722,704	3
KALENŐ	722,712	8
KÁLNA	722,714	6
KÁLNA-ROSZTOKA	See ROSZTOKA (KÁLNA-)	
KAPONYA	722,712	9
KARÁD	722,713	1
KARCSA	722,713	2
KARNÁ	722,714	1
KÁROLYFALVA	722,715	1
KAROS	722,714	2
KASÓ	722,715	2
KÁZMÉR (KIS-)	722,721	1
KÁZMÉR (NAGY-)	722,751	2
KÁZMÉR (OROSZ-)	722,761	2
KAZSÓ	722,714	4
KELCSE	722,715	3
KELECSENY	722,715	4
KEMENCZE (KIS-)	722,721	2
KEMENCZE (NAGY-)	722,752	1
KEREPLYE	722,715	5
KERESZTUR (BODROG-)	722,675	2
KERESZTUR (SZÉCS-)	719,789	2
KESZNYÉTEN	722,716	
KESZTOLCZ, Esztergom county	720,182	2
KIRÁLY-HELMECZ	See HELMECZ (KIRÁLY-)	
KIS- (prefix meaning "little" / See place name without prefix)		
KISFALUD (BODROG-)	722,676	1
KISZTE	722,723	3
KLADZÁNY	722,723	4 labeled as KŁABZÁN
KLENOVA	722,723	5
KOBOLKUT, Esztergom county	720,183	2

KOBULNICZA, Sarós county	722,723	6
KOHANÓCZ	722,724	1
KOHÁNY	722,724	2
KOLBÁSA	722,724	3
KOLBÁSZÓ	722,724	4
KOLBÓCZ	722,724	5
KOLCS-HOSSZUMEZŐ	See HOSSZUMEZŐ (KOLCS-)	
KOLONICZA	722,725	2
KOMARÓCZ	722,725	3 labeled as KOMORÓCZ
KŐRÖM	722,726	3
KÖRTVÉLYES (ALSÓ-)	722,669	3
KÖRTVÉLYES (FELSŐ-)	722,695	2
KOSARÓCZ	722,726	1 labeled as KASARÓCZ
KOSKÓCZ	722,714	3 labeled as KASKÓCZ
KÖVESD (KIS-)	722,721	3
KÖVESD (NAGY-)	722,752	2
KOZMA	722,726	2
KRASZNIBRÓD	722,727	1 labeled as KRASZNIBRÁD
KRASZNÓCZ	722,727	2
KRIVA	722,727	4
KRIVA-OLYKA	See OLYKA (KRIVA-)	
KRIVA (TÓT-)	720,012	3
KRIVOSTYÁN	722,727	3
KRIZSLÓCS	722,728	2 labeled as KRIZAJÓCZ
KRUCSÓ (MAGYAR-)	722,738	1
KRUSCÓ (OROSZ-)	722,761	3
KUCSIN	722,728	4
KUDLÓCZ	722,728	3
KÜLSŐ-BŐCS	See BŐCS (KÜLSŐ-)	
KVAKÓCZ	722,728	5
LABORCZ-VOLYA	See VOLYA (LABORCZ-)	
LÁCZA	722,731	2
LÁCZFALVA	722,731	3
LADMÓCZ	722,729	2 labeled as LADAMÓCZ
LADOMÉR	722,729	3
LASK	722,729	4
LASZTÓCZ	722,730	1
LASZTÓMÉR	722,730	2
LAZONY	722,731	1
LEÁNYVÁR	722,732	1
LEGENYE	722,732	2
LEGYES-BENYE	See BENYE (LEGYES-)	
LELESZ	722,734	
LELESZ-POLYAN	See POLYAN (LELESZ-)	
LESZKÓCZ	722,735	2
LESZNA	722,735	3
LISZKA (OLASZ-)	722,759	1

LOMNA	722,735	4
LOMNICZA (PUSZTA-)	722,735	5 labeled as LOMNICA
LUCZ (TISZA-)	720,006	
LUKA	722,736	1
LUKASÓCZ	722,736	2
LYUBISE	722,736	4
MÁD	722,740	
	722,741	
MAGYAR- (prefix meaning "Hungarian" / See without place-name prefix)		
MAJÓROCZKA	722,738	2 labeled as MAJÓRÓCZ
MAKÓCZ	722,738	3
MAKKOSHOTYKA	See HOTYKA (MAKKOS-)	
MÁLCZA	722,739	2
MÁRK	722,739	3
MÁRK-CSEMERNYE	722,739	4
MASKÓCZ	722,739	1
MÁTYÁSHÁZA	722,739	5
MÁTYÁSKA, Sáros county	722,739	6
MATYASÓCZ	722,738	5
MEGYASZÓ (ALSÓ- and FELSŐ-)	722,742	
	722,743	1
MERNYIK	722,743	2
MEZŐ-LABORCZ	722,744	1
MICSAK, Sáros county	722,744	2
MIGLÉSZ	722,744	3 labeled as MIGLÉCS
MIHAJLÓ	722,744	4
MIHÁLY (NAGY-)	722,753	
	722,754	
MIHÁLYI	722,744	5
MIKÓHÁZA	722,745	1
MIKOVA	722,745	2
MINYÓCZ	722,745	3
MISLINA	722,745	4
MOCSÁR	722,746	1
MODRA	722,746	2
MOGYOROS, Esztergom county	720,184	
MOGYORÓSKA	722,746	1
MONOK	722,747	
	722,748	1
MORVA	722,748	2
MRÁZÓCZ	722,748	3
NAGY- (prefix meaning "big" / See place name without prefix)		
NÁTAFALVA	722,747	2
NECHVAL-POLYÁNKA	See POLYANKA (NECHVAL-)	
NÉMETI (HERNÁD-)	722,705	
NÉZPEST	722,758	2 labeled as NESPEST
NOVOSZEDLICZA	See NOVOSZELICZA	
NOVOSZELICZA	722,758	3

NYÁGÓ	722,758	4
OLASZI (BODROG-)	722,676	2
OLASZ-LISZKA	See LISZKA (OLASZ-)	
OLSINKÓ	722,760	1
OLSVA (ALSÓ-)	722,670	1
OLSVA (FELSŐ-)	722,695	3
OLYKA (HOMONNA-)	722,708	1
OLYKA (KRIVA-)	722,728	1
OLYKA (SZTROPKÓ-)	719,795	2
OND	722,760	2
ORESZKA	722,760	3
ÖRMEZŐ	722,762	1
OROS	722,762	2
OROSZ- (prefix meaning "Ruthenian" / See place name without prefix)		
OSZTRUZSNYICZA	722,761	11
PÁCZIN	722,765	1
PAKASZTO	722,763	1 labeled as PAKSZTO
PÁLFÖLDE	722,765	2
PALOTA	722,763	2
PAPINA	722,763	3
PARIHUZÓCZ	722,763	4
PARNO	722,764	1
PATAK (ARANYOS-)		
PATAK (FEKETE-)		
PATAK (OROSZ-)	722,761	4
PAZDICS	722,764	2
PCSOLINA	722,766	2 labeled as PESOLINA
PELEJTE	722,766	1
PERBENYIK	722,765	3
PETICSE	722,766	3
PETKÓCZ	722,766	4
PETŐFALVA	722,767	1
PETRAHÓ	722,767	1
PETRICK	722,767	3
PETRÓCZ	722,767	4
PETRÓCZ (OROSZ-)	722,761	5
PICHNYE	722,768	1
PISZKORÓCZ		
POJÁNKA (SZTROPKÓ-)	719,796	1
POLENA (NAGY-)	722,752	3
POLENA (SZTROPKÓ-)	719,795	3
POLYAN (LELESZ-)	722,735	1
POLYÁNKA (NECHVAL-)	722,758	2 labeled as NECH-POLYÁNKA
POLYÁNKA (SZÉCS-)	719,796	1 labeled as SZTROPKÓ-POJÁNKA
POLYÁNKA (TAVARA-)	720,000	3
PORUBA	722,768	6
PORUBA (OROSZ-)	722,761	6

PORUBKA	722,769	1
POSSA	722,769	2
POTOCSKA	722,769	3
PRAURÓCZ	722,768	2 labeled as PRAVRÓCZ
PRITULYÁN	722,768	3
PROSZÁCS, Sáros county	722,768	4
PUCZAK	722,768	5
PUSZTA- (prefix / See place name without prefix)		
RÁD	722,770	1
RADVÁNY (HORBOK-)	722,709	3 labeled as HARBOK-RODVÁNY
RADVÁNY (IZBUGYA-)	722,711	5
RAFAJÓCZ	722,770	2
RAKÓCZ	722,770	3
RÁSKA (KIS-)	722,721	4
RÁSKA (NAGY-)	722,755	1
RÁTKA	722,771	1
REGMECZ (ALSÓ-)	722,670	2
REGMECZ (FELSŐ-)	722,695	4
REMENYE, Sáros county	722,771	2
REPEJŐ	722,771	3 labeled as REPELJŐ
REVLEANYVÁR	See LEANYVÁR	
RICSE	719,776	1
ROHOZSNYIK	719,776	6 labeled as ROZSNYIK
ROKITÓ (HOMONNA-)	722,708	2
ROKITÓ (IZBUGYA-)	722,711	6
ROKITÓCZ	719,776	2
ROSKÓCZ	719,776	3
ROSZTOKA, Sáros county	719,776	4
ROSZTOKA (KALNA-)	722,714	7
ROSZTOKA (SZTAKCSIN-)	719,792	5
ROVNA	719,776	5
ROZSNYIK	See ROHOZSNYIK	
ROZVÁGY (KIS-)	722,722	1
ROZVÁGY (NAGY-)	722,755	2
RUDABÁNYÁCSKA	See BÁNYÁCZKA (BUDA-)	
RUDLYÓ	719,777	2
RUNYINA	719,777	3 labeled as RUGYINA
RUSZKA (KIS-)	722,722	2
RUSZKA (NAGY-)	722,756	1
RUSZKA (OROSZ-)	722,761	7
SAJÓHIDVÉG	See HIDVÉG (SAJÓ-)	
SÁMOGY	719,778	2
SÁRA (BODROG-)	722,677	1
SÁROS-KIS-PATAK	See SÁROSPATAK (KIS-)	
SÁROS-NAGY-PATAK	See SÁROSPATAK (NAGY-)	
SÁROSPATAK (KIS-)	719,780	
SÁROSPATAK (NAGY-)	719,781	
	719,782	

SEMJÉN	719,785	2
SITNYICZE (ALSÓ-)	722,670	3
SITNYICZE (FELSŐ-)	722,695	5
SÓKUT	719,786	1
SÓSTÓFALU	722,709	1 labeled as HOPORTY
STEFANÓCZ	719,786	2
SCACSUR	719,786	3
SZADA	720,000	1 labeled as TAKTA-SZADA
SZÁLNIK	719,787	2
SZALÓK	719,787	1
SZÉCS- (prefix / See place name without prefix)		
SZEDLICZKE	719,787	3
SZEGILONG	719,787	4
SZELEPKA	719,787	5
SZELICZA (NOVO-)	See NOVOSZELICZKA	
SZENTES	719,788	1
SZENT MARIA	719,788	2
SZERDAHELY (BODROG-)	722,677	2
SZERENCS	719,788	3
	719,789	1
SZILVÁS-UJFALU	See UJFALU (SZILVAS-)	
SZINNA	719,790	3
	719,791	1
SZINYÉR	719,791	2
SZMOLNIK	719,791	3
SZÖGH	719,791	3
SZŐLLŐSKE	719,792	3
SZOLNICSKA	719,792	2
SZOLOSKE	719,792	3
SZOMOTOR	719,791	4
SZOPKÓCZ	719,792	1
SZTAKCSIN	719,792	4
SZTAKCSIN-ROSZTOKA	See ROSZTOKA (SZTAKCSIN-)	
SZTANKÓCZ	719,793	1
SZTÁRA	719,793	4
SZTARINA	719,793	2 labeled as SZTAZINA
SZTARKÓCZ (SÁROS- and ZEMPLÉN-)	719,793	3 labled as SZTASKÓCZ
SZTASKÓCZ	See SZTARKÓCZ (SÁROS- and ZEMPLÉN-)	
SZTERKÓCZ	See CSABALÓCZ-SZTERKOCZ	
SZTRIÓCZ	719,794	2
SZTROPKÓ	719,794	3
	791,795	1
SZTROPKÓ- (prefix / See place name without prefix)		
SZUHA	719,796	2
SZUKÓ	719,796	3
SZÜRNYEG	719,791	1
TAKSA-HARKÁNY	See HARKÁNY	
TAKSA-SZADA	See SZADA	

TÁLLYA	720,003	2
	720,004	
	720,005	
TAPOLY-HERMÁNY	See HERMÁNY (TAPOLY-ZEMPLÉN-)	
TARCAL	720,001	3
	720,002	
	720,003	1
TÁRCZONFALVA	See TRÁNCZONFALVA	
TÁRKÁNY (KIS-)	722,722	3
TÁRKÁNY (NAGY-)	722,756	2
TARNÓKA (SZÉCS-)	719,790	1
TAVARA-POLYÁNKA	See POLYÁNKA (TAVARA-)	
TECHNA	720,001	1
TELEPÓCZ	720,001	2
TEREBES (TŐKE-)	720,013	
	720,014	
TISZA-LUC	See LUC (TISZA-)	
TOKAJ	720,007	4
	720,008	
	720,009	1
TOKAJ (OROSZ-)	722,761	8
TŐKE-TEREBES	See TEREBES (TŐKE-)	
TOLCSVA	720,009	2
	720,010	
	720,011	1
TOPOLOVKA	720,007	1
TOPOLYA	720,007	2
TOPOLYAN	720,007	3
TORONYA (KIS-)	722,723	1
TORONYA (NAGY-)	722,757	1
TÓT- (prefix meaning "Slovak" / See place name without prefix)		
TÓTH- (same as TÓT-)		
TRÁNCZONFALVA	720,012	5 Labeled as TÁRCZONFALVA
TREPECZ	720,015	1 Labeled as TREPETCZ
TURÁNY	720,015	2
TURCÓC	See TURCZÓCZ	
TURCZÓCZ	720,015	3 Labeled as TURÓCZ
TUROCZ	See TURCZÓCZ	
TUSSA	720,015	4
TUSSA-UJFALU	See UJFALU (TUSSA-)	
UBLYA	720,015	6 labeled as UBJA
UBLYA (BREZOVECZ-)	See BREZOVECZ	
UDVA	720,016	1
UGAR	See UBLYA	
UJ- (prefix meaning "new" / See place name without prefix)		
UJFALU (KIS-), Esztergom county	720,183	1
UJFALU (SZILVÁS-)	719,790	2
UJFALU (TUSSA-)	720,015	5
UJFALU (VÁMOS-)	720,020	1

UJLAK (BODZÁS-NAGY-)	722,678	1
UJLAK (KIS-)	722,723	2
ULICS	720,017	1
UPOR	720,017	2
VAJDÁCSKA	720,017	3
VAJTÓCZ	719,800	3
VALENTÓCZ	720,017	4
VALENTÓCZ and BÉLA (IZBUGYA-)	722,711	1
VALKÓ	720,018	1
VALASKÓCZ	720,018	2 labeled as VAJASOCZ
VÁMOS-UJFALU	See UJFALU (VÁMOS-)	
VAREHÓCZ	720,019	3
VARRANÓ	720,018	3
VARRANÓ-CSEMERNYE	See CSEMERNYE (VARRANÓ-)	
VARRANÓ-HOSSZUMEZŐ	See HOSSZUMEZŐ (VARRANÓ-)	
VÁSÁRHELY	720,020	2
VAVRINYÉCZ	720,019	4 labeled as VAVRICZ
VAVRICZ	See (VAVRINYÉCZ)	
VÉCS (BODROG-)	722,677	3
VÉCSE	720,021	4
VÉG-ARDÓ	See ARDÓ (VÉG-)	
VEHÉCZ	720,020	3
VÉKE	719,798	1
VELEJTE	720,021	1
VELYOPOLYA	720,021	3
VELKROP	720,021	2
VIDRÁNY	719,798	2
VILÁG	719,798	3
VILY	719,799	1
VIRAVA	719,799	2
VISNYÓ	719,799	3
VITÁNY	719,800	1
VLADICSA	719,800	2
VOLICSA	719,800	4
VOLOVA	722,761	9 labeled as OROSZ-VOLICZA
VOLOVA (TÓT-)	720,012	4
VOLYA (JUSZKO-)	722,711	8 labeled as IZBUGYA-VOJA
VOLYA (LABORCZ-)	722,729	1
VOLYA (OROSZ-), Sáros county	722,761	10
ZAMUTÓ	719,801	3
ZÁVADA	719,801	1
ZÁVADKA	719,801	2
ZBOJ	719,801	4
ZBOJNA (HOMONNA-)	722,708	3
ZBOJNA (IZBUGYA-)	722,711	7
ZEBEGNYÓ	719,802	1 labeled as ZEBENYÓ

ZEMPLÉN	719,802	2
ZEMPLÉN-DOBRA	See DOBRA (NAGY-)	
ZÉTÉNY	719,803	1
ZOMBOR	719,803	2
ZSADÁNY	722,670	5 labeled as ARBONYA-ZSADÁNY
ZSALUBINA	719,804	3
ZUBNA	719,804	1
ZUELLA	719,804	2